Women of Achievement

Diana, Princess of Wales

Women *of Achievement*

Abigail Adams

Susan B. Anthony

Tyra Banks

Clara Barton

Hillary Rodham Clinton

Marie Curie

Ellen DeGeneres

Diana, Princess of Wales

Helen Keller

Sandra Day O'Connor

Georgia O'Keeffe

Nancy Pelosi

Rachael Ray

Eleanor Roosevelt

Martha Stewart

Venus and Serena Williams

Women of Achievement

Diana, Princess of Wales

HUMANITARIAN

Sherry Beck Paprocki

CHELSEA HOUSE
PUBLISHERS

An imprint of Infobase Publishing

DIANA, PRINCESS OF WALES

Copyright © 2009 by Infobase Publishing

All rights reserved. No part of this book may be reproduced or utilized in any form or by any means, electronic or mechanical, including photocopying, recording, or by any information storage or retrieval systems, without permission in writing from the publisher. For information, contact:

Chelsea House
An imprint of Infobase Publishing
132 West 31st Street
New York, NY 10001

Library of Congress Cataloging-in-Publication Data
Paprocki, Sherry Beck.
Diana, Princess of Wales : humanitarian / by Sherry Beck Paprocki.
p. cm. — (Women of achievement)
Includes bibliographical references and index.
ISBN 978-1-60413-463-6 (acid-free paper) 1. Diana, Princess of Wales, 1961–1997—
Juvenile literature. 2. Princesses—Great Britain—Biography—Juvenile literature.
I. Title. II. Series.

DA591.A45D535525 2009
941.085092—dc22
[B]
                                   2009008690

Chelsea House books are available at special discounts when purchased in bulk quantities for businesses, associations, institutions, or sales promotions. Please call our Special Sales Department in New York at (212) 967-8800 or (800) 322-8755.

You can find Chelsea House on the World Wide Web at http://www.chelseahouse.com.

Series design by Erik Lindstrom
Cover design by Ben Peterson and Alicia Post

Printed in the United States of America

Bang EJB 10 9 8 7 6 5 4 3 2 1

This book is printed on acid-free paper.

All links and Web addresses were checked and verified to be correct at the time of publication. Because of the dynamic nature of the Web, some addresses and links may have changed since publication and may no longer be valid.

CONTENTS

Just Like a Fairy Tale

The wedding was the social event of the century. The future king of England had chosen as his bride a demure young lady only 19 years old. Yet, she was in the international spotlight as she walked down the aisle at St. Paul's Cathedral in London on that hot summer day in 1981.[1] Lady Diana Spencer was marrying one of the most eligible bachelors in the world: Charles Phillip Arthur George, more commonly known as Charles, Prince of Wales.

London was decked out for the affair, with 4,500 flower-pots lining the route from Buckingham Palace to the church.[2] The pageantry of this royal wedding had not been seen for many years. Carriages made their way from the palace to the cathedral just before noon.[3] Diana rode in a glass carriage drawn by horses to the church where the ceremony would take place.

Meanwhile, at the cathedral, Elizabeth II, the queen of England, arrived in a conservative aquamarine-colored dress. Other princesses, including Charles's sister, Anne, wore dresses in light colors such as peach, yellow, and pink. Charles's grandmother, officially known as Queen Elizabeth, the Queen Mother, wore green.[4] Once everyone had assembled and greeted one another, the royal family was seated near the front of the church.

The wedding seemed like a fairy tale, particularly when Lady Diana arrived in her billowing ivory silk dress with a train that was 25 feet long.[5] More than 2,500 guests filled the church, including royalty from around Britain and throughout the world, the wife of the president of the United States, and many other international figures.[6]

After the ceremony that afternoon, the new bride and her prince joined his royal family on a balcony at Buckingham Palace. Church bells rang out, and the huge crowd cheered as Charles kissed Diana. The royal marriage was official.

A much smaller gathering of 120 guests then attended Buckingham Palace's wedding breakfast, a traditional British wedding reception which featured a fruitcake-style wedding cake that had been baked a month earlier to allow the flavors to meld before the wedding.[7]

The long-awaited wedding for 32-year-old Charles, the Prince of Wales, had finally occurred. He had dated many young women, but not until he met the quiet Lady Diana Spencer did anyone seem appropriate to be the future queen of England. Diana hailed from a royal line herself—there was a king or two somewhere in the Spencer family background. She had grown up near Sandringham, one of the royal family's residences; as a child, she sometimes played games with Charles's younger brother Andrew, who was just a year her senior. Years later, a nanny for one of the children

Britain's Prince Charles kisses his bride, the former Lady Diana Spencer, on the balcony of Buckingham Palace in London, after their wedding on July 29, 1981.

reported that she saw Charles appear once in the library at Sandringham, briefly interrupting a game of hide-and-seek that the younger children were playing with the Queen. Charles was 17 years old at the time; Diana was 5.[8]

Despite having been reared in a privileged environment, Lady Diana did not always lead a happy life. When she was six, her parents divorced. Along with her younger brother, also named Charles, she found herself being transported from their father's home to their mother's home on the weekends.[9]

She grew up in Park House, which was located on the Sandringham Estate. As a child, Diana was known simply as "Diana"; however, when her father became the eighth Earl Spencer and moved the family to the sprawling Althorp Estate, she received the title of Lady Diana Spencer. She was at a boarding school at the time, and she skipped about announcing that she was now Lady Diana.[10]

Diana's introduction to her future husband came through one of her older sisters, Lady Sarah Spencer, who had previously dated Prince Charles. (Charles stopped seeing Sarah after she reportedly discussed their relationship with the press.) After Sarah officially introduced them to each other when Diana was 17 years old, Diana and Charles saw each other only sporadically before beginning to date more seriously when Diana was approximately 19 and working as a kindergarten teacher in London.[11] This pretty young woman was known for her patience and love of children—perhaps that's what the future king of England would need in his new bride. After all, a future queen would have to produce an heir to the English throne.

From the moment that her engagement to Charles was announced on February 24, 1981, the press stalked

DID YOU KNOW?

According to Tina Brown's book *The Diana Chronicles*, Diana's father, the eighth Earl Spencer, served as a personal assistant—officially titled an *equerry*—to King George VI, and for two years to his daughter, Queen Elizabeth II, when she inherited the throne.

Diana. As she dashed in and out of her London apartment, where she lived with three other young women, she tried to hide from photographers who wanted to snap a picture of the future princess. Diana did not know at the time that a troubling relationship with the press would linger throughout her entire life.

Nor did she seem to know the unhappiness that she would encounter after she moved into Buckingham Palace just prior to her marriage. It was a rambling, lonely place, where she attempted to learn the protocol involved with being a member of the royal family. Diana would roam the halls from her second-floor apartment to the kitchen, looking for someone to talk to.

A royal footman—a low-level servant in the palace—once expressed amazement that Diana had wandered into the kitchen in jeans and a T-shirt and buttered a piece of toast for him.[12] There were continuous concerns by some of the royal handlers that Diana was too friendly with the palace staff. "I was afraid her warmth and chattiness might make some of those in the royal service take advantage," said author Stephen Barry, who had formerly served as a member of the prince's palace staff.[13]

Living at Buckingham Palace, Diana was confronted with Charles's extremely busy social schedule. Charles stuck to his daily regiment, attending to royal commitments as well as his hobbies of hunting and fishing. There was, it seemed, little time for the couple to spend together. It was during these early days at Buckingham Palace that Diana first met Camilla Parker Bowles, the woman who is now married to Prince Charles. Rumors persisted throughout much of Charles and Diana's marriage that Charles had an ongoing relationship with Camilla.[14]

Diana also reportedly began suffering from eating disorders during those early years in the castle. Andrew Morton reported that Diana's waist size shrunk from 29 inches at the time of her engagement to 23 inches just before her wedding, barely five months later. "She saw engagement pictures of herself looking heavy, and she promptly went on a diet," said Lady Colin Campbell, author of *Diana in*

EATING DISORDERS

Bulimia and anorexia are two types of well-known eating disorders, although there are other kinds that do not have specific names. Princess Diana suffered from bulimia for most of her adult life.

People with eating disorders have severe eating habits. For example, someone with anorexia nervosa—commonly known as anorexia—will extremely limit the amount of food that he or she eats and will generally eat only certain things. People who suffer from bulimia nervosa may binge eat and then vomit or use other ways to get rid of the food. Those who suffer these disorders tend to feel extremely distressed about their body weight and image. Research is under way to determine why this occurs, but scientists think it has a lot to do with biological, behavioral, and societal influences. Someone who has an eating disorder may also suffer from depression, substance abuse, or anxiety. In extreme situations, people with eating disorders can harm their bodies so much that they eventually die. Therefore, it is important that anyone who develops an eating disorder get treatment as soon as possible.

People with anorexia typically weigh themselves repeatedly and eat only very small quantities of certain foods. In the later stages, anorexics also may have thinning bones, dry and brittle hair, yellowish skin, and other symptoms. To improve their condition, it is important that they return to a healthy weight and get treatment for any psychological issues that may be involved.

Private. This marked the beginning of what seemed to be an ongoing struggle with bulimia for the princess.[15]

Even though Diana was very nervous in the days before the event, the wedding went on as planned. On that

Bulimics eat large amounts of food and usually feel like they have a lack of control over what they eat. Binge-eating is then followed by purging—which can take the form of vomiting or excessive use of laxatives and diuretics. Fasting and excessive exercise are other ways that people compensate for overeating. Someone who is bulimic may have symptoms caused by purging, including intestinal problems and oral decay. Later symptoms may include an ongoing sore throat, swollen glands in the neck, and worn tooth enamel.*

Eating disorders often develop in early adolescence or adulthood; females are much more likely to have them than males. Men and boys account for only 5 to 15 percent of patients with anorexia or bulimia, according to the National Institute of Mental Health. Young people who suffer from either condition should tell a trusted adult who can help them get counseling. A nutritional or psychological counselor can usually treat an eating disorder. Sometimes, family counseling is also necessary.

Additional information about eating disorders, symptoms, and treatments is available at the Web sites of the National Institute of Mental Health (http://www.nimh.nih.gov) or the National Eating Disorders Association (http://www.nationaleating disorders.org).

*"Eating Disorders." Available online at http://www.nimh.nih.gov/health/publications/eating-disorders/complete-publication.html.

beautiful day in 1981, she officially became Diana, Princess of Wales. To people around the world, watching the wedding on television, she seemed to be living a fairy tale life.

In nations such as Great Britain that still honor royal lineage, it is important to have heirs to the throne. Thus, it came as little surprise when, less than a year after her marriage, Diana gave birth to Prince William—a bouncing baby boy who became the second in line to the British throne, just behind his father. Shortly thereafter, the red-haired Prince Harry was born. By all accounts, Diana was a dedicated and responsible mother, even as she grew restless as a member of the royal family. Diana would often surprise her nannies by peeking into the nursery unannounced to see her young sons, who at times were the only joy in her very restrictive life.

Her relationship with the media did not make her feel more at ease. Wherever she went, the press hounded her. "Diana is in the acutely uncomfortable position of being the most gawked-at celebrity," John Skow noted in 1983.[16] The Princess of Wales was one of the most photographed celebrities of her time—a beautiful young mother who wore stylish clothes and was met by throngs of guests wherever she went. Even fellow celebrities wanted to catch a glimpse of her. On a 1985 trip with Charles to the United States, President Ronald Reagan and his wife, Nancy, threw a White House dinner for them. Many celebrities were invited to meet them, including ballet star Mikhail Baryshnikov, actor John Travolta, socialite Brooke Astor, and businesswoman Gloria Vanderbilt.[17]

AN INTERNATIONAL ICON

Diana had become an international icon. She grew in confidence as she went about her public business of meeting dignitaries, as well as spending time with ordinary people.

Prince Charles and Princess Diana and their sons, William *(right)* and Harry, begin a cycle ride around the island of Tresco, one of the Scilly Isles, on June 1, 1989. The royal family was vacationing in the islands, which are located off the southwest tip of Great Britain.

Fashion experts around the world credited her for her poise and elegance.

Yet, for all of her grace in public, Diana's struggles at home continued. Newspaper reports said that she and Prince Charles were drifting apart. There was much speculation about whether the couple would stay married. The more Diana's popularity grew throughout the world, the less it seemed the royal family really liked her. Eight years after getting married, as Charles turned 40 years old, he seemed to want to focus more on his own life. The couple had vastly different interests—she enjoyed shopping, dancing, and playing tennis, whereas he enjoyed polo, long walks, and hunting expeditions.

For a time, they maintained their public appearances despite their personal troubles. The couple, together, received approximately 3,000 annual invitations to charity galas, grand openings, and ribbon cuttings in the 1980s.[18] Although they certainly could not accept all of them, they did their best. By the time Diana arrived in Washington, D.C., in 1990 for a charity benefit, tickets cost $2,500 a person for the opportunity to be in the same room with her. If you wanted to shake hands with the princess, the event organizers charged an additional $1,000.[19]

Wherever she went, people wanted to meet her. Wherever she was, photographers lurked. On New Year's Eve in 1990, Diana was photographed taking a walk by herself along a beach in England. She had escaped the imprisonment of Sandringham Palace, where the royal family was taking a holiday. The photographer who took the photo from several feet away said he was stunned that she had no bodyguards with her.[20]

Despite her loneliness, Diana developed a busy philanthropic life. She is credited with helping the world overcome its initial fear of touching AIDS patients shortly after the disease was discovered in the 1980s. She went to discos in New York and plenty of parties with Sarah Ferguson, the wife of Prince Andrew. As Diana's popularity grew, Charles seemed to sulk at the loss of his own importance. Headlines berated him for not paying enough attention to his two sons and for being an absentee husband.

The more outgoing his princess became, the more seemingly backward Charles appeared to be.[21] When they traveled to Brazil in 1991, they went their separate ways: She visited schoolchildren while he planted a Brazilian nut tree. Thus, it seemed, sadness began to creep into the storybook marriage.

Months after the trip, the couple separated. "The fairy tale had come to an end," Diana said during an interview that was televised around the world in 1995. "It had a huge effect on me and Charles. I felt a deep, deep profound sadness. My husband asked for a separation, and I supported it."[22] Charles, apparently, had once again begun to spend time with Camilla Parker Bowles. Diana later admitted to being involved with a man named James Hewitt, who taught her sons how to ride horses and helped her get over her fear of riding.

By 1996, the "Waleses," as they had become known in the press, decided to divorce at the formal request of Charles's mother. Queen Elizabeth, well known for her reserve and sense of propriety, was tired of the public bickering that was being reported in newspapers around the world. As the royal marriage crumbled, no one seemed sure whether Charles would ever ascend to the throne. Rumors suggested that he might eventually step aside and allow his son, Prince William, to become king.

IN HER OWN WORDS

In a 1995 interview with the BBC, Diana recalled:

> I remember when I used to sit on hospital beds and hold people's hands, people used to be sort of shocked because they said they'd never seen this before, and to me it was quite a normal thing to do.

After the divorce, Diana would retain the title of Princess of Wales and keep her apartment at Kensington Palace. She would also continue to be involved in her young sons' lives. At the time, William was nearly 15, and Harry was 13. During the divorce negotiations, Diana befriended some of England's top reporters, which alarmed the royal household. By reporting ongoing divorce discussions with the royal family, she ensured that the royal family could not disregard her wishes. They could not pressure her into the divorce, or a scant financial settlement, because she was likely to tell the entire world via the news media.

Once a settlement was reached, Diana was on her own. She carved out a new life for herself by trimming down her responsibilities and devoting herself to her sons. Although she now worked with fewer charities, she remained passionately devoted to certain issues, such as ridding the world of land mines that had been left behind from previous wars and helping the sick and wounded. Diana, Princess of Wales, was coming into her own as a humanitarian and an individual. No one knew at that point how little time she had left to live.

A Privileged Childhood

Diana Frances Spencer was born at 7:45 P.M. on July 1, 1961, at Park House, the home of her parents.[1] A simple note in the local newspaper announced her birth a few days later, before her parents had even given her a name.

Diana had a privileged childhood. Her father, called Johnnie Spencer by close friends, was officially titled the Viscount Althorp. Her mother, Frances Roche, was the Viscountess Althorp.[2] Johnnie Spencer would eventually become the eighth Earl Spencer and the landowner of a huge estate called Althorp, which had been handed down within his family from generation to generation.

The Spencers had been a strong and influential family in England for many generations. In 1699, one of the Spencer men married into the affluent Churchill family,[3] which later produced Winston Churchill, the great British prime minister who led his nation through the Second World War and won the Nobel Prize for Literature in 1953.[4] In 1765, King George III had granted an earldom to the Spencer family. That essentially meant that the earl would, for all coming generations, oversee the 14,000 acres of the Althorp Estate.

Diana's father, Viscount Althorp, was the oldest son of the seventh Earl Spencer and was set to inherit the Earl Spencer title when his father died. Until her grandfather died, however, Diana lived with her parents and siblings in a large, rambling Victorian home, known as Park House, which was located on the Queen of England's Sandringham Estate in northern England, not far from the coast of the North Sea.

When Diana was born, she had two older sisters. Sarah was born in 1955, within a year after her parents were married, and Jane was born two years later in 1957. When Diana came along, it has been said that she was nearly over-looked because her parents were so focused on producing a male heir to the Althorp title. Finally, in 1964, Diana's younger brother, Charles, was born and became the official heir to the earldom. The family was elated, and the Queen of England, Elizabeth II, was named his godmother.[5]

In her early childhood, Diana enjoyed fun-filled days playing on the Sandringham Estate with her siblings and other royals who showed up to vacation there—including the queen's son Prince Andrew, who was only a year older than Diana. Sometimes the Queen would visit her royal home at Sandringham and, while out riding horses, stop to talk with the children.

At Park House, servants and nannies looked after the Spencer children; they played with them, spent meal-times with them, and put them to bed. "It was a privileged upbringing of a different age, a distant way of living from

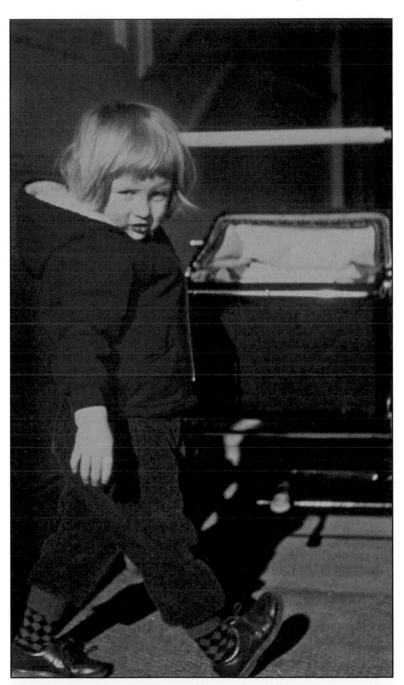

A family-album picture of Diana taken at Park House, Sandringham, Norfolk.

your parents," Diana's brother, Charles, once told the biographer Andrew Morton. "I don't know anyone who brings up children like that anymore."[6]

Park House had 10 bedrooms, a heated swimming pool, tennis courts, a tree house, and a lawn where family and friends played cricket. Although Diana started riding horses when she was three years old, a fall several years later made her afraid to ride. She also developed a fondness for animals of all sizes. She had a cat named Marmalade, as well as hamsters, rabbits, and goldfish. When any of them died, Diana made sure they were given a fond farewell by burying them beneath a huge cedar tree on the grounds and placing crosses on their graves.

With friends and siblings, Diana fed fish in the streams and slid down the banisters of the stairways in her home. She and her siblings learned the basics of reading and writing in a schoolroom on the house's first floor, where their governess taught them. With so much space available at home, the Spencer children were also granted the privilege of establishing a room that memorialized the Beatles, their favorite British band.

CRISIS AT HOME

Once the responsibility of producing a male heir had been met, the marriage between Diana's parents began to deteriorate. Years later, the Spencer children, including Diana, recalled fights between their parents. Diana's mother, Frances—who had married when she was only 18—felt confined at Sandringham and wanted to spend more time in London.[7] When Diana was six years old, her mother gave up her title and left Park House. She assumed that Diana and her brother would be living with her, and she enrolled them in a London school.[8]

Staying with their mother, however, was not meant to be. Diana's father went to court and received custody of the children. He brought them back to Park House and enrolled them in another school.[9] Diana's mother was granted regular periods of visitation.

Eventually, Frances married a wealthy man named Peter Shand Kydd, whose family had owned and later sold a lucrative wallpaper business.[10] What followed were some very sad times for the children. Sarah and Jane were sent off to boarding school, and Diana remembered hearing her brother cry himself to sleep at night at Park House. Sometimes she went to him, but other times she was afraid to get out of bed.[11] Park House could be a scary place in the dark of night, with its rambling windows and long, dark hallways.

Both Diana and Charles told stories of distress regarding their nannies during those lonely years. "Diana and I had a nanny who, when we did something wrong, would bang our heads together, or if one of us did something wrong, would bang our head against the wall," Charles once told a reporter for the *Evening Standard*.[12]

Diana and Charles continued to attend the local school; their father took them and picked them up most days. Diana matured into a quiet and shy girl. On her seventh birthday, her father threw a huge party and brought in a camel from the local zoo.[13] The Spencer children, who shuttled back and forth on the train with their nanny to visit their mother, were showered with wonderful gifts by both of their parents. Yet, the two youngsters seemed to get little of the affection that they so desired. Indeed, what began as a happy, carefree childhood became one that was scattered between two homes and infected with sadness. Many tears were shed whenever the children had to leave their mother to return to Park House.

Diana was nine years old when her father sent her off to a girls' boarding school called Riddlesworth Hall, located two hours from Park House. The years at Riddlesworth

A 1968 family-album photo of Diana with her brother Charles in Berkshire.
Charles became the ninth Earl Spencer in 1992.

were fun and sometimes rowdy. Although Diana joined in
the loud activities in the dormitory, she was shy and quiet
in the classroom. She was not a standout student, but she
worked hard and tried her best. When Diana was 11 years
old, she was saddened by the death of her Grandmother
Spencer. She had always felt close to the woman known as

Countess Spencer, who had watched over Diana since her parents' divorce.[14]

Diana eventually joined her two older sisters at another boarding school named West Heath, which was located in Kent. She much admired her oldest sister Sarah, who was a popular student at the school. (Not until she was a grown woman did Diana became close to her sister Jane, who had also been an excellent West Heath student.) Diana emerged as a bubbly character who often was challenged by her schoolmates to eat hearty amounts of food, only to suffer a stomachache afterward. At West Heath, Diana developed a fascination with history and English, but she also learned about serving those who were less privileged by participating in the school's programs that visited the elderly and the handicapped. In fact, she seemed to excel at working with people who were less fortunate.[15]

When Diana was 14 years old, her father married a woman named Raine Legge, the divorced daughter of the famous British novelist Barbara Cartland. The outgoing and boisterous new wife did not sit well with Diana and her siblings. Charles, who was at boarding school at the time, was told about the wedding by his headmaster the evening after it

DID YOU KNOW?

Diana was never a good student at West Heath Boarding School, and she frequently failed her exams. She excelled, however, at the school's organized service projects, during which students visited elderly, sick, and mentally handicapped people.*

*Andrew Morton, *Diana: Her True Story*. New York: Pocket Books, 1992, p. 37.

occurred. His sisters learned about it when it was announced in the newspapers. Diana was distraught and had some serious words with her father upon learning the news.

Something else happened around that time, too. In 1975, the seventh Earl Spencer died, and Diana's father took over the Althorp Estate. The estate included a stately home of 121 rooms, a vast array of surrounding cottages, and a world-class collection of artwork, silverware, and furnishings.[16] Diana's despised stepmother, Raine, redecorated the home and turned the stable into a tearoom and gift shop that paying tourists could visit. Over the years, the house was renovated further; Diana's stepmother paid for some of the redecoration with the sale of various pieces of artwork and other antiques.[17] When Diana was there, she spent hours in a black leotard practicing the ballet moves she was learning during dance classes at West Heath.

As the future princess finished her education at West Heath, she was given a special award for her community service. She then followed her older sister Sarah to a finishing school in Switzerland, where she was supposed to learn French and the finer skills of sewing and cooking.[18] Although Diana enjoyed the Swiss skiing, she begged her parents to bring her back to England. Eventually, they did.

MEETING CHARLES

Although she had met him briefly as a child, Diana officially met Prince Charles, the heir to the British throne, when she was 17 years old. Her sister Sarah brought him home for a hunting weekend at Althorp. The Spencer family hosted a dinner and dance in his honor, and, although he became acquainted with Diana, Sarah was his official date.[19] Several months later, the budding romance cooled off when Sarah told a magazine reporter that she would never marry anyone she did not love.

Diana's father, the eighth Earl Spencer, and his wife, Raine, in front of Althorp House. Although she loved her father deeply, Diana had a difficult relationship with her father's wife.

In April 1978, Diana was an attendant in her sister Jane's wedding to Robert Fellowes.[20] The following November, both Sarah and Diana were invited to Charles's thirtieth birthday party at Buckingham Palace. Although Charles had another date for the evening, Diana was happy to be there with him. Perhaps it was then that Diana set her sights on marrying the prince.

In the meantime, she wanted to have some fun. For a short time, Diana was a nanny in the Althorp area. After a few months, she convinced her father to allow her to move; eventually she was given a flat in a safe area of London, where she rented space to three of her best friends.

Although she was just 17 years old, the youngest Spencer girl was starting an independent life.

In London, Diana attended a cooking school for three months. For a short time, she taught ballet to toddlers at a school run by her former West Heath teacher. At home, she was a tidy young woman who made sure that the apartment was kept clean and the dishes were done.

In the fall of 1979, Diana became an assistant teacher at a school called the Young England Kindergarten. Several months later, she began to work as a nanny two days a week for an American family who had a nine-month-old son.[21] It was during that time that she seemed to imagine marrying one of the most eligible men in the world, Prince Charles. Just a few years later, in fact, the well-to-do parents of the baby for whom she cared were among her guests at the prestigious royal wedding.[22]

One friend recalled a late night in London, during the months before Charles and Diana began to date, when Diana urged him to drive her around Buckingham Palace a few times. Diana asked her friend if he thought she would ever stand a chance with the prince.[23] To the people who knew her, it seemed that Diana was focused on marrying the royal bachelor, despite their age differences and very different personalities.

A ROMANCE BEGINS

Diana's wish was about to come true. She began to date Charles in earnest when she was just 19 years old. Behind the scenes, her grandmother Lady Fermoy was a good friend of Charles's grandmother the Queen Mother, also known as the Queen Mum. In fact, Lady Fermoy had the official title of the Queen Mother's Woman of the Bedchamber.[24] These two older women thought their grandchildren would make a good match, and they set out to help the future king of England find his queen.

Because of their discussions, perhaps, Diana reportedly began to receive more invitations to attend the theater, the opera, and other events that included the prince and his friends. During the summer of 1980, she was invited to a house party by some of the prince's friends. More events and activities followed in the fall. Charles invited Diana to attend a performance of Giuseppe Verdi's *Requiem,* and her grandmother went along as a chaperone. After the performance, the three of them went to Buckingham Palace for dinner.[25]

A few months later, Diana joined Charles for a weekend aboard the royal yacht. Later, at a weekend retreat at the Queen's Balmoral Castle, Diana was watching Charles fish when she saw three photographers lurking in the bushes. She hid behind a tree to get out of their range, but the word was out. The press knew about the prince's new girlfriend.

In November 1980, the press began to stalk Charles in earnest as he celebrated his thirty-second birthday. Some years earlier, he had suggested that he might marry in his early thirties. Was Diana the girl he would marry? There seemed to be no settling down yet, however. As he drove to a farm on the Sandringham Estate, he sped in front of a pack of photographers in his expensive Aston Martin sports car.[26]

Charles spent his birthday afternoon foxhunting on horseback with his usual royal entourage. The press had congregated outside of Diana's flat, hoping to catch a glimpse of her, but she tricked them by leaving especially early in the morning.[27] The news of a pending engagement did not come, despite the hopes of the photographers who spent the day waiting and watching. "I cannot go anywhere without being recognized," Diana once commented to reporters. "I am followed everywhere."[28]

In the months that followed, Charles took Diana to the house he had just purchased. It was another sprawling home, called Highgrove, with nine bedrooms that sat on 347 acres. Diana was surprised when Charles suggested she begin decorating it.[29]

On February 6, 1981, Charles invited Diana to join him for a quiet dinner at Windsor Castle. It was there that he proposed and reminded her that, if she accepted, she would one day become the Queen of England. At first, Diana giggled. Then she quickly accepted his proposal. When she was presented with a tray of potential engagement rings, she selected a large sapphire surrounded by 18 smaller diamonds.[30] Charles then went to call his mother to tell her the good news.[31] The heir to the throne would soon be married, and all of Great Britain would celebrate.

Diana left London soon after to spend time with her mother and stepfather in Australia, where her stepfather, Peter Shand Kydd, had a sheep ranch. Charles understood Diana's need to get away. "I wanted to give her a chance to think about it—to think if it was all going to be too awful," Charles later told a reporter.[32] When Diana returned from Australia, an official palace announcement was scheduled. Diana and her mother chose a powder-blue suit from Harrods, a well-known British department store, for the future princess to wear for the very important day.

The Queen and her husband, Philip, the Duke of Edinburgh, joined the happy couple for the announcement. They were in the grand ballroom of Buckingham Palace when the announcement was read: "It is with the greatest pleasure that the Queen and the Duke of Edinburgh announce the betrothal of their beloved son, the Prince of Wales, to the Lady Diana Spencer, daughter of the Earl Spencer and the honorable Mrs. Shand Kydd."[33]

Diana's sister Sarah took credit for bringing the couple together. "They just clicked," she told newspaper reporters. "They have the same giggly sense of humor, and they both

ALTHORP

The burial site of Diana, Princess of Wales, is at the Althorp Estate in northern England. The estate contains 14,000 acres of land, including cottages, farms, and even small villages, but 550 acres of Althorp are within a walled park that surrounds the Spencer family home, known as Althorp House. The estate has belonged to the Spencer family for 500 years, and 20 generations have lived there.

When Diana visited her father, the eighth Earl Spencer, during breaks from school, she liked to tap dance in the ornate Wootton Hall. Although she had always found Althorp stuffy when her grandfather lived there, she appreciated it more as she grew older.

Diana's younger brother, Charles, became the ninth Earl Spencer when his father died in 1992. He then moved into Althorp with his own family. Although many people are employed to help him, Charles works hard to take care of the family home, like his father did before him. He rents out some of the rooms in the home as a way to help pay for necessary repairs and upkeep. Among the rooms available for rental are the Great Room, where 30 people can be seated for dinner, and the State Dining Room, which seats 120 people.[*]

Upon Diana's death, her brother insisted that her body be returned to Althorp so that her final resting place could be well protected. Diana's burial site is on a tiny island in a small lake on the Althorp estate. Although Diana's gravesite is very private and peaceful, the house at Althorp is open to visitors who want to see its extensive collection of art and historic furnishings.[**]

---

[*]"Althorp Hospitality." Available online at http://hospital.althorp. co.uk.
[**]"Althorp Living History." Available online at http://www. althorp.com.

love ballet and opera and sport in all forms. It's perfect, they are both over the moon about it."[34]

Palace historians immediately announced that Diana would become the first English woman to marry the heir to the throne in more than 300 years. During that time, most heirs had sought spouses outside of England.[35]

Diana's fairy tale life, it seemed, was about to begin. In a matter of months, she would ride in a historic glass coach to St. Paul's Cathedral, where she would marry the man of her dreams.

The Royal Wedding

Diana was thrilled. Even though she knew her life would be forever changed, this shy and quiet young woman thought her dreams of a fulfilling and meaningful future were about to come true. Little did she know, however, how challenging her life would become. Wherever she went, she was stalked by photographers trying to get a photo of the soon-to-be Princess of Wales.

When Diana returned to her apartment the evening that Charles proposed, she excitedly told her roommates, who promptly popped open a bottle of champagne.[1] A few weeks later, before the engagement was publicly announced, she left the apartment and moved into Charles's grandmother's living quarters in London. There, she was given tips and advice that were supposed to help her adapt to royal life.

Later, Diana moved into her own apartment at Buckingham Palace, the primary residence of the Queen of England when she stays in London. A huge home of 775 rooms,[2] it consists of a labyrinth of hallways and corridors that are lined with historic furnishings and artwork by some of the world's great masters. Some people might think that living there is akin to living in a museum. Although areas of the palace are open for public events, its public rooms are few in contrast to the mammoth operation required to take care of the royal family. The palace is home to many butlers, maids, electricians, and plumbers; it even has a post office and a doctor's surgical room.[3]

ISOLATED AND ALONE

With several months to go before the wedding, Diana felt lonely and isolated in the palace. Because each member of the family had a private apartment at Buckingham Palace, Diana saw little of the royal family. She no longer worked as a nanny or a kindergarten teacher; her new job was to learn how to be a member of the royal family—and she found the days long and often boring. Sometimes she wandered the palace halls, chatting with staff or visiting the kitchen for a snack. According to royal protocol, this behavior was considered extremely inappropriate. The staff was not supposed to interact with the royal family; in fact, they were supposed to stay out of their view altogether.

Eventually, Diana began to entertain herself by listening to music, wearing headphones as she walked the palace hallways. Living inside the palace was very different from what she had originally imagined. No one, it seemed, really paid much attention to her while she was there. Her personal suite, which had been home to Charles's royal nanny years earlier, included a bedroom, a bathroom, and a kitchen.[4] It was there that she spent many days, alone, leading up to the wedding. Yet despite being isoloated inside the place, photographers followed her wherever she went outside the palace walls.

It fell to royal servants to protect Diana from the public, the press, and the millions of admirers she began to gain throughout the world. Yet, few friends and only some of her family were able to visit the soon-to-be princess. "It was as though she had been whisked off to an ivory tower . . . never to be seen again," one of Diana's former roommates told journalist Tina Brown.[5] As a result of her loneliness, Diana began to make friends among the palace staff—a move that, again, was considered very inappropriate.

In the meantime, preparations for the royal wedding continued. Although the Queen sent thousands of invitations, Diana was allowed only 100 invitations for friends. Her parents each received 50 invitations for their close friends and family members. Even Charles was only allowed 300 for his personal use.[6]

Weeks before the wedding, Charles went on a planned tour to Australia, New Zealand, Venezuela, and the United States and was gone for five long weeks.[7] Again, this left Diana feeling awkwardly alone in the massive palace where she now lived.

Eventually, Diana scheduled lessons with her former dance teacher. The time she spent in her black leotard, moving easily across a room, was probably a form of relaxation for the young woman who would soon have the eyes of the world on her. In the days that led up to the wedding, Diana fretted that Charles seemed to ignore her at times. Her photo often appeared in the press, which made her more self-conscious. Diana began to think that she was too fat, and she developed bulimia as a way to control her weight. People close to her worried that she was growing too thin. Even the seamstress who made her wedding dress fretted that it would look too big on the wedding day.[8]

Everyone waited with great anticipation for the wedding of the century. The stress was building, and few knew how nervous Diana felt about having the eyes of the world on her as she walked down the aisle to marry her prince. A few weeks before the wedding, as she watched Charles play polo, Diana burst into tears; the press snapped photos that would be published around the world the very next day. Her fiancé seemed to understand and blamed the constant media attention for much of Diana's anxiety while she attended his matches. "It's not much fun watching polo when you are being surrounded by people with very long lenses poking at you from all directions the entire time and taking a photograph," Charles said during an interview a few days later. "So I hope after we get married it will be a bit easier for her to come to a polo match without this intensity of interest."[9]

Despite all of the media attention, little was known about Diana's feelings of anxiety in the days leading up to the big event. In public, she generally looked happy. In private, she was in turmoil. She was unsure of the role she needed to play as the new Princess of Wales. She felt very alone, even though she was about to marry one of the most sought-after men in the world.

The youthful Diana was very much in love with the sophisticated older prince, but it seemed she had no way of communicating with him. Many years later, she remarked that they had seen each other on dates only 13 times before they were married.[10] Charles was often busy with his official duties and preoccupied with his sports and travels. In the days that led up to the wedding, she generally called him "sir"—the way one would traditionally address a royal. Diana wondered if the wedding might be just another royal obligation to him. Only the coming years would tell the truth.

Charles himself hinted that his busy life might make it difficult to have a wife and family. "It's the most difficult thing trying to work out how you can have a family life as well as all the public demands there are," he once said during a television interview. "I tend to lead a sort of idiotic existence trying to get involved in too many things and dashing about. And this is going to be my problem, trying to sort of control myself and, you know, work out something so that we can have a proper family life."[11]

Diana broke free of her youthful style of dressing during one of the few dates with her fiancé. Her usual frock was a blouse or suit that featured a ruffle at the neck. On this particular date, she stunned royal watchers as she stepped out of a limousine that had taken them to a musical recital in London. Diana was wearing a black taffeta dress with a low neckline.[12] Suddenly, it seemed, people were stunned to see her looking so elegant and beautiful. This event was the beginning of Diana's role as a fashion icon. As it turned out, the black dress was a fashion faux pas; Diana later discovered that royals usually wear black only to funerals. Yet, she did not seem to care. "Black to me was the smartest color you could possibly have at the age of nineteen," she said in an interview. "It was a real grown up dress."[13]

Nearly a week before the wedding, Diana and Charles gave a television interview. They were seated in wooden garden chairs in a sunny summerhouse situated on the Buckingham Palace estate. Charles admitted being overwhelmed by the support they had received. He mentioned that more than 3,000 gifts and 100,000 letters had arrived since their engagement was announced. "There's a corridor stacked with them," he said. "I don't know, 40 sacks of presents and mail which we can't get through."[14]

U.S. president Ronald Reagan and his wife, Nancy, sent an expensive glass bowl made by the Steuben glass company. From her home in Texas, the former American ambassador to Britain, Ann Armstrong, sent western boots for Charles and chaps for Diana. A German company sent

$20,000 worth of kitchen accoutrements.[15] As gifts arrived at the palace, each one had to be checked out by a security specialist to ensure it was safe. Then it was catalogued for future reference.[16]

For the interview, Diana—who was quickly becoming known for her fashion sense—wore a matching gray and white skirt and a ruffled blouse. She said that she was already busy writing thank-you notes. The young royals had registered at two of London's top stores for wedding gifts, and they had already received everything on their lists.

The soon-to-be princess, nicknamed "Shy Di" during her engagement, told her prince during the interview that she was just becoming more comfortable with the press coverage of their big day. "I don't know about Diana, but I'm more used to it," Charles said. Throughout the months of their engagement, Charles frequently expressed concern to his friends and staff members that so quickly becoming part of the royal family would be too difficult for Diana.[17] When one of the interviewers asked Diana if Charles had been helpful during this adjustment period, she replied: "Marvelous. Oh, a tower of strength."[18]

The royal couple made several appearances together in the weeks that led up to the wedding day, including another couple's wedding and a film premiere. Diana stole much of the attention when she was a guest at the Queen's summer garden party.[19] On July 1, 1981, she celebrated her twentieth birthday with a small family dinner at Buckingham Palace—the same day that the palace announced official proceedings for her and Charles's forthcoming wedding.[20]

All of London seemed caught up in the wedding preparations. Two young designers named David and Elizabeth Emanuel worked on Diana's dress, which featured antique lace embroidered with pearls and sequins; a thin, body-hugging waist; and a memorable 25-foot train that barely fit into the glass carriage on the day of the wedding. At the same time, Charles and Diana chose the music for their ceremony—he chose a George Frideric Handel hymn called "Let the Bright Seraphim," and she chose a patriotic hymn called "I Vow to Thee, My Country."[21] The royal baker worked hard to create the massive fruitcake that would age before it was served at the post-wedding breakfast. Milliners worked diligently on hats ordered by royal guests, and London's gardens were prepared for the world to see as it watched the wedding.[22]

On the Monday before the big day, Diana knew that Charles was having lunch with Camilla Parker Bowles, an old friend with whom he had once been romantically involved. She worried that Charles would continue seeing Parker Bowles and that there was more to their relationship than just friendship. Even though Parker Bowles was now married with children of her own, Diana knew that she had been one of Charles's first loves.

While Charles visited with his former girlfriend, Diana entertained her older sisters for lunch at Buckingham Palace. She was seriously considering canceling the wedding, she told them. She was unsure of Charles's love for her, and she was disillusioned about royal life as she now saw it. Diana did not know if marrying the prince was what she really should do. Her sisters, however, did not seem to take her too seriously. "Bad luck, Dutch," they told her, using her childhood nickname. According to Andrew Morton, they told her that it was too late to call off the wedding.[23]

The evening following the luncheon with her sisters, Charles and Diana hosted a celebratory ball at Buckingham Palace for 800 of their close friends and family. European royalty attended, as did First Lady of the United States Nancy Reagan, and British Prime Minister Margaret Thatcher.[24] Diana wore a ravishing pink gown and a necklace of diamonds and pearls. By all accounts, it was a rowdy affair—Princess Margaret, the Queen's younger sister and Charles's aunt, even attached a balloon to her royal crown.

After the ball, Diana was taken to the Queen Mum's Clarence House for her final night before the wedding. Charles watched celebratory fireworks over Hyde Park while 250 musicians provided sound effects[25] and 101 bonfires that had been planned burned on hilltops throughout the English countryside.[26]

That same evening, Charles sent Diana a kind note that said, "I am so proud of you and when you come up the aisle I'll be there at the altar for you tomorrow. Just look 'em in the eye and knock 'em dead."[27]

THE WEDDING

Diana woke up early on the morning of July 29, 1981. The crowd began to grow out on the Mall. People had come from near and far to watch the royal procession, which would include Diana in a glass carriage as well as other carriages to take the royal family to the church. A hairstylist, a make-up artist, and the dress designers were there to help her prepare for the event that 750 million people around the world would watch.[28]

Her father waited for her at Clarence House, and together they climbed inside the glass carriage for the ride to the cathedral. The two-mile parade route to the church was heavily guarded by 7,000 policeman and British soldiers.[29] Finally, the future princess stepped from her carriage, grabbed her father's arm, and entered the church.

The bell in the church tower struck 11:00 A.M., and the organist started to play a song called "Trumpet Voluntary." Diana, the fairy-tale princess, began her slow procession to the altar.[30] According to English tradition, five little girls were asked to be bridesmaids. One of the bridesmaids was Princess Margaret's daughter, Sarah Armstrong-Jones.

The Princess and Prince of Wales wave from their carriage on their wedding day, July 29, 1981, as it makes its way across London. Millions of people around the globe watched the "fairy-tale wedding" on television.

Stitched into Diana's flowing silk gown was a tiny good-luck charm: a golden horseshoe studded with diamonds.[31]

"She was never one for make-up but she did look fantastic," her brother Charles later said. "It was the first time in my life I ever thought of Diana as beautiful. She really did look stunning that day and very composed, not showing any nerves although she was slightly pale. She was happy and calm."[32]

As Diana was led down the aisle by her father, who was still recovering from a recent stroke, she looked around for familiar faces among the crowd of nearly 2,500 people.[33] She saw her sisters; her younger brother, Charles; and her mother and stepfather. Her former roommates sat in the first row.

She saw the royal family: Charles's sisters and brothers, the Queen, and her husband. Her eyes also found Camilla Parker Bowles, and she hoped that her husband-to-be had forgotten about his past relationship with this now-married woman.

Then she focused on Charles, her prince waiting for her at the altar in the full dress of a Royal Navy commander. He was joined by his brothers, princes Andrew and Edward, who were his attendants. As the ceremony began, Diana made somewhat more modern vows to her prince, electing to remove the word *obey* from her statement. "Marriage is the kind of relationship where there should be two equal partners, and if there is going to be a dominant partner, it won't be settled by this oath," noted Dr. Edward Carpenter, the dean of Westminster Abbey, who had performed other royal marriages.[34]

The ceremony—slightly more than an hour long—was broadcast to television stations around the world by the British Broadcasting Corporation (BBC) from 21 cameras set up inside the church. One camera was even anchored at the top of the church's dome and recorded dramatic video as the bride walked down the aisle with her father at her side.[35]

According to a report that was published in *Time* magazine a week after the ceremony, translators provided commentary for the ceremony in 34 languages.[36] Tina Brown, who was then the editor of London's *Tatler* magazine and many years later wrote *The Diana Chronicles*, was hired as a royal expert by NBC's *Today* show to provide commentary to American viewers.[37] "England's tiny social magazine was suddenly in the middle of the biggest tabloid story in the world," Brown later wrote.[38] In an era when many publications still did not produce color photographs, this "wedding of the century" inspired some to commit to the extra expense. The *Times* of London produced a souvenir edition; the newspaper published a color photograph of the royal couple on its front page. For the first time in its 138 years of existence, the British intellectual magazine the *Economist* also printed a color news page.[39]

Indeed, the eyes of the world watched as this young woman became the fairy tale princess. Even in countries that do not have royal families, such as the United States, people were infatuated with the affair. Some in the media questioned the relevance of Britain's royal family, which has no significant power and are little more than figureheads. "There are those who are positive about the monarchy, and those who are lukewarm," a politics professor from the University of Strathclyde in Scotland noted when questioned. "There aren't many anti people."[40] The summer that the young royals took their vows was a difficult one for British politics. Unemployment was high, a growing restlessness began among citizens, and riots occurred. Yet many Britons considered the wedding to be great news. "The royal family is good for the country," said one young man. "It gives the country a focal point, a bit of stability."[41]

When the Archbishop of Canterbury concluded the wedding ceremony, he told his large audience:

> May the burdens we lay on them be matched by the love with which we support them in the years to come. However long they live, may they always know that when they pledged themselves to each other before the altar of God they were surrounded and supported not by mere spectators but by the sincere affection and active prayer of millions of friends."[42]

Then he proclaimed them man and wife. Hearing the proclamation on speakers outside the church, the crowds roared.

The wedding party departed the church, and this time Diana rode with Prince Charles as they proceeded back
(continues on page 46)

KENSINGTON PALACE

Although Kensington Palace was built in 1605, it did not become a royal residence until 1689, when it was purchased by King William III and his wife, Mary. The royal couple had previously lived at a riverside palace called Whitehall, but because King William suffered from asthma, the damp and mildewed location affected his health. Once the couple purchased their new home, which was called Nottingham House by its previous owner, they made renovations to accommodate the royal household.

The royal couple had four additions built onto the building's four corners. Each addition was four stories and included an attic. A new entrance and a service courtyard also were added. When King William went to war against the Irish, his wife extended her quarters and built a separate block of rooms for her servants.

In 1908, sunken gardens were added to the palace grounds to re-create the landscape that surrounded Kensington in the seventeenth century. The gardens flourish from April to October every year with plantings that reflect the season. An ornamental pond is the centerpiece of the gardens.

When Princess Diana lived at Kensington, from 1981 until her death, her quarters were in the west wing of the building— both while she was married and after she divorced. Her apartment remains part of the royal family's residence.

Recently, the palace opened a display that features 12 of Diana's dresses, including one that she wore to a dinner at the White House in Washington, D.C., in the 1980s. The night she wore that sparkling dark-blue gown, the crowd gathered around to watch her disco dance with John Travolta. (Diana sold 79 of her gowns at a charity auction in 1997, including the blue dress that is currently on loan for display at the palace.)

A photo of Kensington Palace in London, which was Princess Diana's official home until her death in 1997.

Because there are other residents in the palace, Diana frequently felt like she was being watched by the other members of the royal family who lived there. Today, three of Queen Elizabeth's cousins and their families reside at Kensington. Other residents include Prince and Princess Michael of Kent, the Duke and Duchess of Kent, and the Duke and Duchess of Gloucester. The employees of the royal household who work for Queen Elizabeth and Prince Charles also have their living quarters at Kensington Palace.

Although residential areas of the palace are kept private, including Diana's former apartment, public areas are open nearly every day of the year, except for the Christmas holidays. Areas that visitors can see include the King's Gallery, where artwork

(continues)

(continued)

is displayed, and Queen Victoria's bedroom, where she awoke in 1837 to discover that her uncle, the king, had died. The Orangery is an eighteenth-century restaurant where Kensington visitors can still have tea and a light lunch.*

---

*"Kensington Palace." Available online at http://www.hrp.org. uk/KensingtonPalace.

(continued from page 43)

to Buckingham Palace for the Queen's planned breakfast. Minutes after they disembarked from their carriages, the royal family appeared on a palace balcony. There, the prince kissed his new bride, which he had not done during the ceremony.[43]

Then the parties started. The wedding party and close family participated in the Queen's breakfast, while other guests were invited to a lunch given by Prime Minister Margaret Thatcher. Later that day, a soireé was thrown by Lady Elizabeth Shakerly, a friend of the royal family. At this event, scrambled eggs and bacon were served to guests who arrived at the ballroom of a London establishment called Claridge's.[44] Around London and the English country-side, other, smaller events also were planned, including an English barbecue in an Oxfordshire village and a reenactment of the royal wedding in Tetbury.[45]

For Diana, all of the celebration seemed much bigger than the young girl who was at the heart of it all. Diana, Princess of Wales, was about to begin a new life as a royal.

An Heir
and a Spare

Following the wedding breakfast at the palace, Charles and Diana drove off in the prince's dark blue Aston Martin to spend a couple of days at an estate called Broadlands. Then they headed off for a two-week Mediterranean cruise on the royal yacht *Britannia*.[1] The yacht made periodic stops in ports along the way. Eventually, the honeymoon cruise ended when Diana and Charles left the yacht in Egypt and flew on to Australia.[2]

At this time, Diana, who was now officially known as Her Royal Highness, the Princess of Wales,[3] was like a butterfly coming out of its cocoon. Although she still privately struggled with bulimia,[4] the shy Diana had blossomed into a graceful young woman. Unlike most members of the royal family, who did not necessarily want to be fashion trendsetters, Diana drew a lot of attention wherever she went with her fashionable clothes. Sometimes, however, she was embarrassed to find she received more attention than her husband. Though Charles was a dashing young husband, and the future king of England, it was his new wife who drew all eyes as they traveled about meeting and greeting crowds of people.

Women all over the world loved Diana. They started to style their hair the same way that Diana did. They admired the young princess's clothing, her jewelry, and her worldwide status. Soon after the wedding, designers began to copy the pattern of Diana's wedding gown so that future brides could buy one of their own.[5] To many women, it seemed like a dream to be looked after by a palace staff of ladies in waiting and other such employees of the royal family.

After the wedding, Diana and Charles moved into an apartment in Kensington Palace in London. Some of their wedding gifts stayed there, but others went to Charles's royal retreat called Highgrove, which he purchased months before the wedding. The gifts numbered in the thousands and included, among other things, a bedspread that the queen of Tonga had knitted herself. A ton of peat was sent from a district council in England, most likely for Charles to use on his Highgrove lawn or in the gardens. A complete bedroom suite arrived from Canada,[6] along with so much more.

Diana much preferred to spend time in London than at the rural Highgrove Estate. She was frequently bored at Highgrove, even though the spacious home had been redecorated and its garden newly landscaped. Charles loved to ride his horses or work in his garden, but Diana preferred their London apartment at Kensington Palace.[7]

Certainly, the young princess stayed busy. It was estimated that she had approximately 170 official royal

Charles and Diana pictured aboard the royal yacht *Britannia* at the start of their honeymoon cruise.

obligations a year, including her attendance at the opening of the British Parliament, the Royal Ascot race, the Chelsea Flower Show, the Wimbledon tennis tournament, and more garden parties than anyone could count.[8]

When she traveled abroad, Diana took a lot of luggage. Sometimes she needed more than 50 bags to accommodate the many outfits she wore each day.[9] Princess Diana did not need to work; her job was to make special appearances on behalf of the royal family. Money for her wardrobe and other expenses came from Charles. According to news

reports at the time they were married, Charles had an estimated wealth of $450 million dollars. The British govern-
ment paid him a salary of $1.25 million a year, but he gave
about half of that back to the government.[10]

By some press accounts, during her first year of marriage, Diana spent about $2,500 a week on clothes. Perhaps
the outfits she wore as a kindergarten teacher no longer fit
her needs. She convinced Charles to begin wearing brighter
ties and less somber suits. She even convinced his hair styl-
ist to let his hair grow a bit longer.[11]

Charles worried about his young bride and the stresses
of leading such a public life, especially with regard to the
media attention that she received. Yet perhaps he should not
have been so concerned. Despite the challenges involved,
during the early days of her marriage Diana refined her
relationship with the press. (Later, it was discovered that
she leaked details of the royal family's private life to some
of England's best reporters.) "I love working with children,
and I have learned to be very patient with them," Diana
once told Charles before they were married. "I simply treat
the press as though they were children."[12]

GROWING POPULARITY

Diana's popularity continued to build after their wedding.
On an autumn tour in 1981, the royal couple spent three
days in Wales introducing the new princess to the throngs of
people who gathered to greet them. Charles and Diana drove
100 miles along the country's north coast in a motorcade of
13 cars and shook thousands of hands with residents along
the way. "We want Diana," the crowd chanted whenever the
cars stopped. Diana, the first Princess of Wales since 1910,
was formally introduced to the Welsh people.[13]

Although Diana was extremely popular during their
travels around the world, when she was back at the palace
no one seemed to pay much attention to the newest

member of the royal family. The attention the media gave Diana continued to grow, but the young princess received little advice from the palace about how to deal with it. After all, nearly everyone else had been born into the royal family. In the beginning, everyone thought the media would eventually lose interest in Diana, but that did not happen. She received more and more attention wherever she went.

In public, Diana was a shining star. In private, however, she still faced many challenges. Even in the early months of her marriage, she worried about Prince Charles's continuing interest in Camilla Parker Bowles. She still felt lonely and isolated inside the palace or the other royal homes, and Charles followed a schedule similar to the one he had followed as a bachelor. She worried that the man she loved did not love her back.

Charles was a fairly spoiled young man himself. As the future king of England, the prince was used to being easily accommodated, no matter his whim. His royal staff made sure that his days went well and that he was always comfortable. If he wanted to hunt and fish, his wish was granted. If he wanted to go horseback riding, the day was devoted to his desires. As part of his royal duties, Charles frequently made special appearances around the world, but Diana expected him to be the Prince Charming of her dreams.

As a result of Diana's insecurities, she and Charles frequently argued. Finally, the prince suggested that she get counseling. Several psychologists and doctors visited the palace, in an attempt to help Diana deal with the rigors of her new royal life.[14]

Diana's life continued to change. When she and Charles had been married for only a few months, rumors began to spread that the princess was pregnant. Indeed, she took her duty of producing an heir to the throne rather seriously, and the rumors were proved true when Diana's pregnancy was officially announced. Three months into her first pregnancy, Diana became extremely ill with morning sickness and fell down some steps at the Sandringham Estate. Doctors were immediately called, but Diana and the baby she was carrying were pronounced healthy.[15]

The young and pregnant princess seemed to be continually depressed. Some reports suggested that she had attempted to commit suicide on numerous occasions, including her fall down the steps at Kensington Palace. Perhaps it was an extraordinary amount of emotional turmoil caused by her pregnancy or perhaps it was all of the major changes going on in her life. No one seemed to know for certain. Whatever the root cause, the royal family was concerned with the health of the new princess.[16]

Nonetheless, the couple that had many struggles between them in private were about to become parents in a very public way. Their baby—a son—would be no ordinary child. He would grow up to be the king of England, following in his father's footsteps. Thus, all of the world awaited the birth.

In February 1982, Charles and Diana took a relaxing trip to the Bahamas. Though they desperately sought privacy, they were photographed on the beach by the press photographers who constantly hounded them. Queen Elizabeth was reportedly livid when she saw one of the photos in a London newspaper—Diana, five months pregnant, in a bikini, putting suntan lotion on the prince's back.[17] "I've never done anything so intrusive in my life," the photographer admitted years later.[18] There would be no peace, it seemed, for the soon-to-be royal parents.

PRINCE WILLIAM

Finally, the big day arrived. At 9:03 P.M. on June 22, 1982, Prince William Arthur Charles Louis was born.[19] Crowds

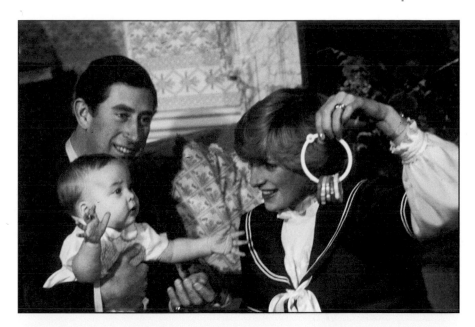

Pictured, Charles and Diana with their son Prince William during a photo session at Kensington Palace in December 1982. Unlike other royal parents, who gave their children to nannies to rear, Charles and Diana were very involved with the day-to-day lives of their sons.

that had gathered outside of St. Mary's Hospital in London popped open bottles of champagne and broke into song. "For he's a jolly good fellow," they sang loudly.[20]

Diana's father was the first to talk to the press, who anxiously awaited the official word of the birth. "Diana is very well, and so is the baby," he announced. "I've spoken with Charles and he's absolutely over the moon."[21]

Eventually, Charles—who had been with Diana throughout the delivery—left the hospital. He joked with the press that the baby was lucky that he didn't look like his father.[22] The new Prince William, who weighed slightly more than seven pounds,[23] was nearly perfect. His parents waited almost a week before they finally agreed on a name, and then it was formerly announced by Buckingham Palace.[24]

The birth of Prince William had a dramatic impact on the succession to the throne. Charles's two brothers, princes Andrew and Edward, as well as his sister, Princess Anne, all moved down one place on the list. After Charles had his turn at being the king of England, Prince William would be next in line—no matter his age.

Even though Diana was only twenty years old—her twenty-first birthday was not for another few weeks—she had done what no other woman in England at the time could do. She had successfully produced a male heir to the throne. In the media, much discussion took place about the tiny baby's new name. Britain's first King William was the Duke of Normandy, who captured England in the year 1066 and thus became known as William the Conqueror.[25]

People in Great Britain and across the world rejoiced. Forty-one-gun salutes were scheduled at Hyde Park and the Tower of London to celebrate.[26] The mood was celebratory—poems were written and souvenirs were created to commemorate the birth of this beloved child.[27] The fairy-tale royal couple now became the perfect royal parents—at least that is what people thought.

Already, Charles and Diana had hired a royal nanny—a 39-year-old woman would take care of the new baby due to his parents' very busy schedule. Unlike royals of the past, however, Diana wanted to keep the baby near her at night instead of sending him to the staff's wing of the palace. Diana felt that she knew what was best for her child.

Immediately after the baby's birth, Diana was elated. She loved being a mother and spending time with her baby. Charles, too, was very taken with his new son—he changed his diapers and became involved in other ways. Eventually, though, exhaustion and bulimia began to take a toll on Diana. Once again, she struggled. She cried. She worried about the baby's health. She feared that Charles was still seeing Camilla. Even though the new days of motherhood should have been worry free for a princess who lived in a towering palace, for Diana they were not. She was severely depressed and, once again, received psychological counseling.[28]

In the meantime, the media was not kind. Photographers snapped pictures of Diana when she left the palace to shop or meet friends for lunch. Media reports called her a "shopaholic" and said she was too controlling of Prince Charles.[29] Diana, it seemed, was losing favor with the press. Disgruntled palace staffers were fired and moved on. The word around London was that Diana had changed. In truth, this young mother was still attempting to adapt to the rigors of her royal life.

It became apparent that the media had begun to turn on her. "She should be brought up short," one British gossip columnist told a reporter for *Time* magazine. "The message got through to Diana that she cannot behave badly and that she'd better start pulling up her socks. Since then, she has been out all day, visiting hospitals and talking with children. She is showing more interest in Charles' hobbies. She is wearing the same clothes over again."[30]

Nonetheless, photographers continued to stalk Diana wherever she went. News of her eating disorder eventually made it in the press, and royal watchers noticed that the princess was getting very thin. Even though stories were wrong at the time—they called Diana's disorder anorexia and not the bulimia she later admitted to having—it was still startling news for the world to read. "Is It All Getting Too Much for Diana?" asked one headline in a London newspaper.[31] Meanwhile, discussion among the media noted that if Prince Charles were to divorce his unhappy princess, he would give up his right to become king. The entire country, it seemed, was concerned with the royal marriage.

Diana broke protocol in 1982 when she refused to leave baby William behind as she and Charles traveled to Australia. Thus, an invitation arrived at the palace inviting them to bring the baby, too. For four weeks, William and his nanny stayed at an Australian home while the royal couple traveled the countryside. Every few days, they returned to spend time with their new child. Because the arrangements worked out so well, Charles and Diana toured New Zealand for an additional two weeks.[32]

Though she was exhausted and preferred to be with William, Diana was the hit of the trip. Huge throngs of people gathered along the streets to greet the Prince and Princess of Wales. Again, Charles was often ignored while his wife received most of the attention. All of the focus on Diana seemed to take its toll on him. Although she loved her husband very much, it seemed that Diana could do nothing to make him as popular as she was with the people who came from miles around to see them.[33] Despite her depression and ongoing battle with bulimia, she still dazzled the crowds.

In private, Diana had little time to spend with any close friends. Seeking companionship wherever she could find it, she became close to the men who served as her royal bodyguards. She considered some of them very good friends, even though they were hired by the palace to watch over her. Because she felt she could confide in them, she was able to hide her depression from the old friends and family members who knew her best.

PRINCE HARRY

Following trips to Canada and France, more news arrived: Diana was pregnant again. "I had a feeling she would put off having another baby for a while," wrote a surprised Stephen Berry, who was Prince Charles's personal valet for 12 years, in his book *Royal Secrets*. "She most certainly did not enjoy being pregnant. She used to mutter that if men had the babies there wouldn't be any."[34]

Once again, she had morning sickness and struggled to keep up with her daily schedule. On September 16, 1984, at 4:20 P.M., Diana gave birth for a second time. Her 6-pound, 14-ounce son, Prince Henry Charles Albert David—better known as Harry—became the third in line to the British throne behind his father and older brother.

Charles stayed with Diana throughout the delivery, which was conducted at the same hospital where William was born. When he left the hospital a few hours after the birth, he joked with the members of the press who had gathered: "We have nearly got a full polo team now."[35] Diana's father was also very happy. "All went very well," reported Earl Spencer from his home at Althorp. "I think the person who will be very pleased will be Prince William, because it will be wonderful for him to have a little companion and a playmate."[36]

Diana left the hospital with Charles at her side just 22 hours after the baby was born. Wearing a red coat and carrying the tiny baby in a bundle, she was greeted by about 1,000 people who had gathered outside the hospital. "Hurray, Harry!" they shouted as the princess blushed.[37]

Prince Harry's birth ensured the line of succession to the British throne—thus, the moniker that Harry was given. His birth completed the phrase that royal watchers use: his brother is the heir to the crown, and he is the spare.

The People's Princess

Prince Harry was just a year old when Charles and Diana took a widely publicized trip to the United States. The royal couple had spent much of the previous year visiting other countries and attending charities in Britain as they built their reputation as one of the most glamorous couples in the world. When they visited the United States, the children did not accompany them.

All eyes were riveted to the tall and slender Diana on the night of Saturday, November 9, 1985. Wearing a dark blue, glittering ball gown, she was about to make a huge splash at a White House dinner in Washington, D.C. Charles and Diana were being honored by President Ronald Reagan and his wife, Nancy, at a star-studded affair with many celebrities in attendance, including

The Princess of Wales dances with the actor John Travolta at the White House, as President Ronald Reagan and Mrs. Nancy Reagan *(in white)* look on.

John Travolta, Clint Eastwood, Neil Diamond, and Tom Selleck.[1]

At dinner, Diana sat next to famed Russian ballet dancer Mikhail Baryshnikov. They chatted quietly while eating lobster mousseline with Maryland crab and glazed chicken capsicum, and a dessert of peach sorbet. Other celebrities in attendance included renowned architect

I.M. Pei, explorer Jacques Cousteau, and socialite Betsy Bloomingdale. President Reagan gave a toast, and Charles did too—although he nearly forgot to do so when his turn came![2]

After dinner, Travolta invited Diana to dance. The actor was well known for his lead role as a dancer in the movie *Saturday Night Fever*, which helped launch the disco era of the late 1970s. When he and Diana walked onto the dance floor, the rest of the crowd backed away to watch. The two performed a stunning disco dance number that people talked about for many years to follow. "She's a good dancer," reported Travolta a few days later. "She's got style and rhythm."[3] When another reporter asked Charles what he thought of the dance, he said, "She'd be an idiot if she didn't enjoy dancing with John Travolta."[4]

The royal couple was in America for several events, though the presidential dinner received the most media coverage. Their worldwide popularity was on display when more than 4,000 people greeted their plane when it landed at Andrews Air Force Base near Washington. After she emerged from the plane, Diana spent nearly 20 minutes talking with a 16-year-old boy from Mississippi who had traveled to Washington to meet her on a trip sponsored by the Make-A-Wish Foundation. The teenager had an inoperable brain tumor and was already blind.[5]

The couple stayed at the British Embassy in Washington, and their three-day trip included a visit to the National Gallery of Art's show called "The Treasure Houses in Britain," to which Charles had lent a painting.[6] A few days before the Saturday evening dinner, they had met the Reagans at a get-acquainted event that included tea and toast. While Charles visited the American Institute of Architects on another day, Diana went to a home for the elderly, where she talked with about 40 residents, many of whom were in wheelchairs.

The morning after the White House dinner, the royal couple visited the Washington Cathedral, where Charles read scripture during the service. They had lunch at the Virginia estate of philanthropist Paul Mellon and later attended a dinner at the British Embassy. There, Diana was resplendent in a long-sleeved, cream-colored evening gown with lace at the top and a taffeta skirt. She also wore a tiara of diamonds and pearls—an item she did not normally wear.[7]

On Monday, their final day in the city, Diana visited a drug rehabilitation center in nearby Virginia while Charles visited the Library of Congress. That night, they were guests at a gala at the National Gallery. The following morning, they flew to Palm Beach, Florida, where Charles played polo. Later that evening, they were honored at a ball at the Breakers Hotel, one of the most glamorous places in town. Tickets to the event were $10,000 per couple and benefited one of Charles's favorite causes, the United World College Fund. It was something of a birthday celebration, in fact, as Charles turned 37 years old that week.[8]

HOME AGAIN

Although it was an exhausting trip for Diana, the 24-year-old princess and mother had made quite a splash in the United States. She had easily socialized with international politicians and celebrities and seemed to have captured the hearts of the many Americans who gathered at each place that she visited, either alone or with Charles. When she returned to the United Kingdom, she continued her busy daily schedule but still found time to play with her two toddlers in the gardens at Kensington Palace. William—known as "Wills"—was now three years old and attended nursery school in a quaint Victorian home in London's Notting Hill section.[9] Whether they were at Kensington or Highgrove, Diana would pop in and out of the nursery to check on the boys, who were with their nanny. William was reportedly turning into an ornery little boy; press reports claimed that he attempted to flush shoes down the toilet for fun.[10] It was not unusual for Diana to get out of bed to check on the boys if she heard them unable to fall asleep—even though royal mothers in the past had allowed the nannies to handle such situations. "A mother's arms are more comforting than anyone else's," Diana once said, apparently recalling her own, lonely childhood.[11]

Charles, by all reports, was also very involved in his sons' upbringing. Sometimes he bathed the children and played with them. He desired to be a more in-touch father than his own father had been to him.[12] Although Prince Phillip seemed to be very proud of his son, he was never involved with Charles's childhood day-to-day care.

Around the palace, Diana had acquired a reputation for being somewhat bossy. More than 40 employees left—some because they wanted to, and others because they were fired. When Diana issued orders, she wanted to be sure that the staff followed through. Overall, Diana was still bored with life at the palace and preferred to be out. When she went out, she generally made a scene and had a swirl of activity surrounding her every appearance. At one London charity ball, she wore a barebacked silver gown and danced until 2:30 A.M. A few weeks later, she went to a ball at a country house in England and danced until 4:00 A.M. Usually Charles was elsewhere.[13]

HER CHARITY WORK

Despite her love of social events, Diana stayed very active in charity events around Great Britain. No other members of the royal family, it seemed, made themselves more available to the charity circuit. She became the president of Barnardo's, a charity that looked after troubled children. She was also the guest of honor at an elaborate event that became known as the Tiffany Ball, which raised money for the AIDS Crisis Trust.[14]

In the early 1980s, acquired immunodeficiency syndrome (AIDS) had just been identified as a specific disease. As some medical researchers attempted to find its cause, others began to actively look for a cure. Medical professionals and families who watched loved ones die from the disease were stunned with its rapid spread around the world. At the beginning of the AIDS health crisis in the 1980s, people often avoided touching anyone who had contracted the disease. Few people knew its causes, and many were afraid they could get the disease merely by shaking hands with an infected person.

AIDS charities would have growing significance to Diana. During a visit to the first AIDS ward in the United Kingdom in 1987, she decided to shake hands with a dozen AIDS patients—and the British media was impressed that she did it without wearing gloves. "She gave it respectability and a profile," said a professor who focused on the AIDS epidemic at Middlesex.[15] "HIV [the virus that causes AIDS] does not make people dangerous to know, so you can shake their hands and give them a hug: Heaven knows they need it," Diana said.[16]

Although she felt ignored by the royal family, Diana came to realize that, outside the palace walls, her star power could help unleash millions of dollars in donations to help those in need. She began to attend as many charity events as possible. In addition to helping raise money at these events, Diana also spent hours in hospitals visiting the sick and dying, as well as in homeless charities visiting those in need. Her mere presence often brought comfort to people she touched.

THE MODERN PRINCESS

Some critics blamed the palace staff for keeping Diana from getting closer to Charles. Royal protocol, they argued, kept the couple distant and prevented the monarchy from modernizing its outlook through Diana's influence. "The circle of unappealing men who surround Prince Charles

AIDS

Acquired immunodeficiency syndrome, or AIDS, is the final stage of a disease caused by the human immunodeficiency virus (HIV). HIV attacks a person's immune system so that he or she is susceptible to a range of illnesses, which can sometimes lead to death.

Researchers first started to notice HIV and AIDS in 1981 but could not find its root cause. At the time, its victims were chiefly homosexual men and intravenous drug users. At the beginning of the AIDS epidemic, many people died because of the disease. People who had the disease were isolated and alone; few people would risk their own health to be close to them. As Diana began to visit AIDS victims in the late 1980s, she helped others get over that stigma, as photos of her comforting AIDS victims in Britain appeared around the world.

Meanwhile, progress was being made by researchers. Although there is still no cure, drugs have been developed that help control the HIV infection and may delay the onset of AIDS.

Today, more than one million Americans and more than 33 million people around the world live with HIV/AIDS.[*] There is no way of knowing if a person has HIV until he or she is medically tested. The disease is primarily transmitted by having unprotected sex (sex without a condom) with someone who already has the virus or through blood-to-blood contact, such as sharing a needle to inject drugs. The virus can enter another body through any exchange of bodily fluids. If a baby's mother has AIDS, the child can be infected during pregnancy, birth, or while breastfeeding.

may dismiss her as 'barmy' because in their world, it is simply insane to be so emotional," explained one feminist writer. "They do not see that what Diana does, that what

Years ago, people who received blood transfusions were at great risk of getting the virus, but today all blood donations in the United States are tested for the virus before they are used. The Centers for Disease Control recommends that a person gets tested once a year if he or she engages in behaviors that can transmit the HIV infection. Those behaviors include injecting drugs with used needles, having sex for money or drugs, having sex with an HIV-infected person, having more than one sex partner, and having a sex partner who has had several partners before you.

If a person is diagnosed with HIV, the patient can remain healthy by following a doctor's advice and making sure he or she keeps medical appointments; takes prescribed medication; gets immunizations to prevent pneumonia, flu, and other diseases; quits smoking and using drugs; eats healthy foods; exercises regularly; and gets enough sleep. The only completely effective way for a person to prevent HIV/AIDS infection is to not have sex until he or she is in a committed relationship (and to ensure that his or her partner tests negative for the infection if that person has had previous partners) and to not use a dirty needle or syringe. The use of another person's razor or toothbrush should be avoided as well, because it may have blood on it.

*"Fact Sheets and Brochures." Available online at http://aids.gov/prevention/factsheets/index.html.

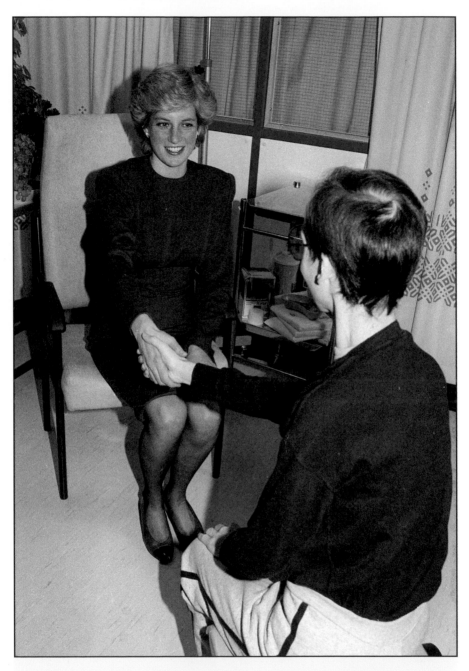

Diana shakes hands with an unidentified 32-year-old AIDS patient in his private room at Middlesex Hospital, London, on April 19, 1987. The photographer was asked not to photograph the patient's face.

she embodies, in a way that Charles never can, is modernity itself. Diana is a modern woman, with the aspirations and problems that face many women today."[17]

As one might expect of the next king of England, Charles was well guarded by the men who looked after him, but did these men prevent Charles and Diana from growing closer? Diana's loneliness seemed to subside a bit once she introduced a young lady named Sarah Ferguson to her brother-in-law Prince Andrew. "Fergie," as Sarah later became known in the press, was a red-haired, fun-loving girl, the daughter of Prince Charles's polo manager, Major Ronald Ferguson.[18] At the request of Queen Elizabeth, Diana invited Sarah and another single woman named Susie Fenwick to the Royal Ascot race. Apparently, the Queen thought it was time for her younger son to find a wife. Although Prince Andrew had dated many girls in the past, none seemed quite suitable for the royal family.

This was not the case with Sarah Ferguson. Sarah accepted the invitation to the Royal Ascot weekend and was greeted by a footman when she arrived at the castle. There, she was shown to her room by one of the Queen's ladies-in-waiting. Once she settled in, she discovered the entire weekend schedule, as well as seating charts for various meals and such.[19] Apparently, Diana was unaware that the Queen's intent was to find a royal match for Prince Andrew. Perhaps the Queen had an ulterior motive as well—perhaps she knew that the young Princess Diana would benefit from having a good friend inside the royal life. Whatever the Queen's reasons, with the help of Diana's friendship, Fergie seemed to integrate into the royal family fairly easily. In fact, it seemed that Sarah Ferguson was better accepted among the royal family than Diana ever had been.

Diana had known Sarah Ferguson for many years. The two were actually fourth cousins and had seen each other occasionally since childhood. Sarah had attended the wedding of Charles and Diana, and she had invited the new princess to her London apartment at times.

Although Sarah helped Diana's loneliness, the princess still suffered from psychological problems. A few months after Sarah's introduction to Andrew, Diana fainted during a royal appearance while she and Charles were traveling abroad. Her bulimia was back in full force; the princess had not eaten much in days. She recovered somewhat and joined the prince on a visit to Japan before returning to her everyday life at Kensington Palace.[20]

Eight months after they met, Sarah and Prince Andrew were married. It was a lavish affair, though not as important in British circles because Prince Andrew was now only fourth in line for the throne. (Following the births of William and Harry, his status had dropped.) Still, Diana and Fergie had a lot of fun—they even dressed as policemen on the night of Prince Andrew's bachelor party and met him at the Buckingham Palace gate when he returned.[21] As royal watchers around the world began to notice, Fergie's influence on Diana created changes in the royal princess. She began to go out more and enjoyed parties with Sarah's friends. With them, Diana was more herself than she could be around the palace.

Diana's obsession with living a happy royal life seemed to be waning, however. At this point, she assumed that Charles continued to see Camilla Parker Bowles. At least Diana now had a good friend with whom she could travel, go to discos, and share secrets. Although her marriage seemed to be growing more unhappy, the balance she sought in her life seemed better than perhaps it had ever been before. After all, she was a popular princess known throughout the world, and her little boys were happy and charming. Still, there were pieces of her life that she knew were missing: She desperately wanted love from Charles and acceptance by the royal family.

Around the world, discussion continued about whether Charles and Diana had a happy royal marriage. "Although they are always in the public eye, very little is known of their personal lives or feelings," Jo Thomas reported in the *New York Times*. "Every shred of information about them, however trivial, is pondered at length. . . . But some of the recent reports have been rather unkind, including published reports that the royal couple argues a lot, that he is eccentric and henpecked, and that she is obsessed with clothes and diet."[22] To combat these allegations, the royal couple appeared on Britain's Independent Television News (ITN). "Well, yes, I think I'm becoming more eccentric as I get older, probably," said Charles during the interview.[23]

As Diana's profile rose around the world, it seemed that Charles—though perhaps not eccentric—was almost in hiding. He worked in his gardens more. He fished and hunted. He painted watercolors, which he claimed to be a therapeutic hobby.[24] (One of his early paintings, done when he was a child, was of his mother's coronation and was given as a gift to his nanny. Eventually, the painting was sold by the esteemed Sotheby's auction house.[25]) Charles seemed to make fewer public appearances—but perhaps it only appeared that way because the media covered his wife's activities more than his own. No longer, however, did he seem proud of the attention that his wife received. Although the royal couple still appeared in public together, they seemed to have little in common. Years later, Diana admitted in a videotaped conversation with a speech instructor that she had had an affair with a man named James Hewitt, an accomplished horseman who had given her, William, and Harry riding lessons.[26] Hewitt later betrayed the princess when he wrote his own book and talked of the affair. The princess, it seemed, was unable to trust anyone who came into her life.

A Marriage in Ruins

It had been five years since Diana, the Princess of Wales, visited Washington, D.C., with Charles and joined John Travolta on the White House dance floor. In 1990, she returned to Washington on her own. This time, Diana would appear at an exclusive event to benefit the ballet dance groups of Washington and London. In addition, she planned to spend time at a charity called Grandma's House, which was a home for children with AIDS.

Diana's star power had only increased in the years between her visits. Tickets for the ballet gala were priced at $2,500 per person. "You have to be an AIDS patient or have 10 million dollars to meet her in America," Roxanne Roberts reported in the *Washington Post*. "There's no way for the middle class to see her. It's not the embassy's fault;

organizers hijack the royals for their rich and powerful friends."[1]

By this time, Diana had appeared on the cover of *People* magazine 43 times. Everyone in America knew who she was. "She's a fairy tale come true," said the magazine's publisher. "She personifies all those fantasies little girls have about being a princess. You just couldn't help get caught up in it."[2]

For the gala event, flowers were shipped in fresh from Holland, and caterers were flown in from London. The menu included filet of beef, green beans, and fruit cups; the champagne flowed. Gold chairs matched the gold china for the 250 people in attendance. Ten footmen in eighteenth-century costumes greeted the guests as waiters served dinner wearing gloves and tuxedos.[3]

Though her marriage had grown more and more unhappy, Diana still reigned in the eyes of her fans. As beautiful as ever, she drew admiration throughout the world, particularly among young people. On a trip to Australia with Charles, Diana was thrilled to visit with children. "It's just heaven being with children again," she told an employee at the school that she visited.[4]

Yet, her popularity also meant that everyone seemed to be talking about her unhappy marriage. *Ladies' Home Journal* printed a cover story titled "Is Diana Happy?"[5] It was an interesting question to ask. As part of a royal family that had hundreds of servants, 24 homes, a fleet of yachts, and 14,600 horses, one would not expect her to be unhappy.[6] Diana, however, was finding out that all of those servants, homes, and vacations were meaningless without a true sense of belonging.

Many people—both inside the palace and in the media—wondered what Diana had to be unhappy about. Perhaps it was her ongoing struggle with depression that made her unhappy—or perhaps it was her need for reassurance from a husband who was too busy with his own life to pay much attention to her. The princess eventually sought therapy to combat her bulimia, after being encouraged by one of her former roommates who had grown terribly concerned about her thinness. "I did what I would do to any close friend who was very ill," explained Carolyn Bartholomew in a news report that was filed a few years later. "I made her understand that she had to get the best doctor possible for her condition."[7] At the same time, Diana turned to aromatherapy, massage, and other new age methods to find happiness in her life.

Meanwhile, Charles continued to follow his own wishes and desires. In the spring of 1990, 57 of his watercolors were part of a one-man exhibit that he held in a small Italian village. "I am not exhibiting sketches under the delusion they represent great art or a burgeoning talent," the prince said at the time.[8] Still, the critics were not kind. "This is a sorry, even unpleasant, little exhibition," said one.[9] Little was heard about Charles's hobby of painting after that event.

When Prince Charles fell from a pony during a polo match in 1990, Diana left an opera performance in London and rushed to his side. The injury required surgery, but Diana's attendance at his bedside was brief.[10] Instead of spending time with Charles, who did not seem to be very interested in her company, she visited with other patients. Charles recuperated with his own friends around him. "She has come across as someone who has suffered from very low self-esteem and has been deeply hurt," a marriage counselor later wrote in a column for London's *The Mail* newspaper.[11]

DIANA AT 30

In 1991, Diana turned 30 years old. She no longer was the demure young woman who had married her Prince

Charming. Diana seemed to have overcome her lack of self-esteem to grow into a self-assured woman who was not only a princess but also a mother to two growing boys. A London society columnist called her a "stunning success."[12] At least, that was the case in her public life.

"She has this extraordinary natural talent," explained the columnist.[13] Diana even received accolades for taking her royal job so seriously, working long hours as she greeted a wide variety of crowds. Although people sometimes talked about her lack of a formal college education—even calling her an "airhead"—others thought she was an exemplary example of a working mother.[14]

That same year, the Queen of England turned 65 years old. There was much discussion about whether she would abdicate the throne—retire and allow Charles to become king of England.[15] As the prince awaited the day that he would become king, his popular wife waited too, as she traveled the world—both with and without him—as an unofficial ambassador for the royal family. In 1992, she traveled to Hungary to meet Croatian refugees who had escaped the Bosnian War—a civil war that later became an international conflict. She went to India and visited the sick and dying people at a hospice where Mother Teresa worked. A few months later, she was in Egypt, where she posed in front of the pyramids.[16] Certainly, Diana kept very busy as she awaited the next turn in her life.

In reality, it would have been very unusual for Queen Elizabeth to abdicate the throne. After all, when she became queen as a young woman in 1952, it was a job she knew she would have until she died. "She's never given any indication that she will step down, and I don't think she will," said one professional royal watcher at the time. "It would go against everything she believes in."[17]

Other marriages among royal family members were struggling, too. In March 1992, it was announced that

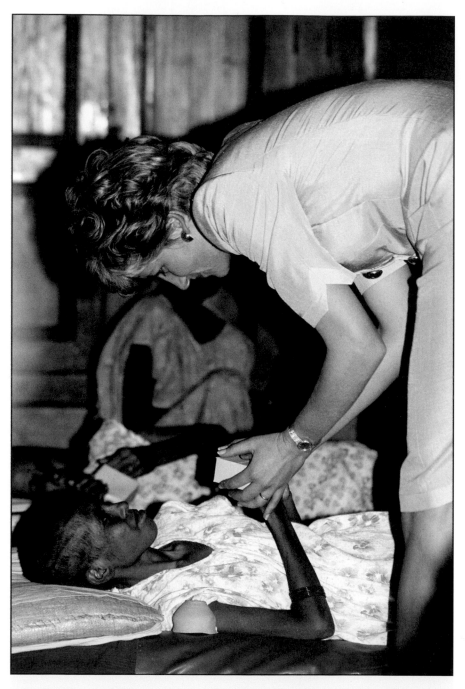

On a trip to India in February 1992, Diana comforts a dying woman at Mother Teresa's hospice in Calcutta.

Sarah and Prince Andrew, known as the Duke and Duchess of York, would separate.[18] Charles's sister, Princess Anne, had divorced during the summer and planned to marry someone else.[19] In a public address, Queen Elizabeth remarked on the difficult year: "1992 is not a year in which I will look back on with undiluted pleasure."[20]

FATHER'S DEATH

In March 1992, Diana's father died at the age of 68 in a London hospital after suffering a heart attack. Although Charles and Diana lived very differently most of the time, they still vacationed together with their children. Thus, at the time of her father's death, Diana was with Charles and their sons on a ski vacation in Austria; they rushed home when they heard the news.[21] Before they left Austria for London, Charles attempted to comfort a distraught Diana on the balcony of their hotel. "Why don't you just leave us alone?" she yelled at photographers below.[22]

Her father's death meant that Diana's younger brother, Charles, would become the ninth Earl Spencer, and he and his wife and their children would move into Althorp, with its expansive collection of artwork and traditional furnishings. Diana and her siblings had been somewhat upset that their stepmother, Raine Legge, had sold some of Althorp's furniture and art to finance a renovation of the estate.[23] As soon as their father died, however, Raine left the estate.[24]

Meanwhile, Diana had begun to discover that the royal marriage was not her dream come true. There was continual discussion in the British media and among royal watchers about whether the marriage of Charles and Diana would survive. Accusations surfaced regarding alleged affairs, and phone conversations were recorded and leaked to various members of the media. Some even thought that, because of Diana and Charles's marital discord, the monarchy was in peril. They feared that the British people would decide they had no use for a royal family.

By the time that Andrew Morton's biography *Diana: Her True Story* was released in 1992, the whole world knew that there was trouble at the palace. In addition to other subjects, the book reported on Diana's continual bouts with bulimia. Eventually, it was revealed that the book had a positive effect on the public by bringing eating disorders into more open discussion.[25]

The biography also addressed Diana's multiple suicide attempts and her ongoing unhappiness with her marriage and the royal family. The book, which quoted some of Diana's best friends, certainly portrayed a princess in peril. It seemed apparent that this was a woman who could no longer live within the confines of the palace walls. Eventually, it was revealed that the princess herself had cooperated with Morton by providing tape-recorded interviews that she had with an intermediary.[26]

The royal couple's problems continued to be discussed in the media. Despite having two children together, it was apparent that Charles and Diana were a bad match. "It's

IN HER OWN WORDS

In a speech about eating disorders given in April 1993, Diana admitted:

> Eating disorders, whether it be anorexia or bulimia, show how an individual can turn the nourishment of the body into a painful attack on themselves and they have at their core a far deeper problem than mere vanity.

clear that Diana prefers the company of the more spirited members of the Travolta generation," wrote one reviewer who had also penned a book about the survival of the British monarchy.[27]

Charles, however, was in a desperate situation—fearing, perhaps, that an end to his marriage would mean never becoming king. Meanwhile, Diana told the biographer and others that she never felt as though she would become England's queen.

It seemed, however, that Britain's royal family had no rules in place that required Charles to stay married. "Lawyers say the unwritten British constitution lets the royals do more or less as they please with their private lives—so long as no monarch weds a Catholic and the heir is legitimate," explained one news report.[28]

THE END OF A ROYAL MARRIAGE

By the end of 1992, the word was out: The Prince and Princess of Wales would officially separate. On December 10, just over 11 years since the two had married, they agreed to end their unhappy marriage. Prince William was 10 and Prince Harry was 8. "This decision has been reached amicably and they will both continue to participate fully in the upbringing of their children," said Prime Minister John Major in a nationally televised news conference, in which he spoke to Britain's House of Commons.[29] On the day the announcement was read, both royals went about their work. Diana visited a clinic in northeast England, and Charles was in London to visit nursing homes and address a business luncheon.[30]

Queen Elizabeth had helped the two come to agreement. After several months of public bickering between the royal couple, the Queen seemed to give up and decide to allow Diana and Charles to live apart. Still, questions remained. "Can the ancient protocols and traditions of the monarchy accommodate the tricky conventions of marriage and family in the 1990s, with the special demands of single parenthood and joint custody?" asked the writer of an article in the *New York Times*. "Even trickier, will the royal couple be able to date other people?"[31]

In the meantime, people in Britain wondered about Diana's role if Charles became king. The title of "Queen Consort" was suggested when Major addressed Parliament on that fateful December day.[32] Nonetheless, this was not an immediate concern: Charles would not become king anytime soon—perhaps never. Amazingly, there was no modern protocol for a royal divorce; the last British king whose marriage had dissolved was George IV in 1796.[33]

As if to reassure the British that Charles could still be king, the archbishops of Canterbury and York released a joint statement, which said that the separation would not affect Charles's future position as head of the Church of England, a position that would be granted to him upon becoming king. Even though the church frowned on divorce, it did not have a rule against it.[34]

IN HER OWN WORDS

In a speech given in December 1993, Diana asked the public to grant her some privacy:

> I hope you can find it in your hearts to understand and to give me the time and the space that has been lacking in recent years.

The week before their separation was announced, Diana went to Highgrove. With the help of her sister Lady Jane Fellowes, the princess told her sons about the separation with their father. Later, she loaded up her belongings so that she could move permanently to her apartment at Kensington Palace.[35] Despite her royal separation, the princess would still be allowed to live in a palace because she was the mother of the future king of England. Certainly, Diana benefited from being the wife of the prince. Her separation agreement reportedly granted her $1.55 million a year as well as a staff.[36] Meanwhile, Charles maintained his home at Highgrove and would use apartments at his grandmother's home, Clarence House.[37]

The British media was in a frenzy, reviewing the details of the unhappy marriage and predicting what would happen in the future. The morning after the official announcement, Britain's *Sun* newspaper ran 26 pages of stories about the royal separation.[38]

Christmas 1992 was a lonely one for Diana. She had lost her father and her husband. She spent the holiday with her brother, Charles, and his wife at Althorp, while her two young sons were with Charles and the rest of the royal family on their annual sojourn to Sandringham.[39]

A Jet-Setting
Philanthropist

Diana knew that she needed to get her personal life on track. Her personal trainer recommended a voice coach who could help her give better speeches. She spent months with the voice coach, during which time she confided some of her most intimate thoughts to him.

"Before, she was tending to do speeches that were either documents written by someone else or 'I'm delighted to be here' speeches," the coach said. "Those ones made her into a bimbo. She didn't want to be treated as a bimbo. She wanted to be treated as though she'd got a brain."[1]

The speech coach became a friend to Diana. He started to record her on a video camera, and they discussed what she was passionate about. Their meetings went on for more than a year, and during that time he helped her figure out what she next wanted to do with her life. "She wanted to be heard," he said. "She needed to be heard."[2]

The spring following her separation from Charles, however, Diana announced that she would scale back her work on behalf of the approximately 80 charities that she favored.[3] Some people thought that Diana had been pressured by the royal family to slow down and stop making so many appearances. Rumors abounded that the family did not want Diana to continue overshadowing Charles. "She has simply lost the battle with the big guns at the Palace," said one London newspaper. "They have been gnashing their teeth at the way she has stolen the limelight from the established royals."[4]

Whatever the reason, Diana's life did slow down. Perhaps she really needed a break. The previous month, Diana had been spotted crying in public. "Twelve years ago, I understood that the media might be interested in what I did," she said when her hiatus from public life was announced. "But I was not aware of how overwhelming that attention would become, nor the extent to which it would affect both my public duties and my personal life, in a manner that has been hard to bear."[5]

In the meantime, Diana had formed a close relationship with the man who helped her sons learn to ride horses. Major James Hewitt also helped Diana overcome her fear of riding horses, which began following a fall she had experienced as a child. Later, Diana admitted in taped interviews with her speech coach that she and Hewitt had been romantically involved. Around the same time, Prince Charles admitted that he and Camilla Parker Bowles were also involved. By 1994, Hewitt had written a tell-all book about his affair with the princess—a revealing look that deeply hurt Diana.

During the next few years, Diana made new friends. One of her confidantes was the wife of the Brazilian ambassador, first to Britain and later to America. Lucia Martins Flecha de Lima was 20 years older than Diana and perhaps offered her the maturity and nurturing that Diana's own mother did not. In 1994, Diana spent the summer at Martha's Vineyard with de Lima, where her host arranged for her to swim in private pools and use private beaches around the island to avoid the paparazzi. In the following months, Diana visited her friend a few times in Washington, D.C. The two also traveled internationally together, going to Indonesia at least once.[6]

Diana's schedule of palace-endorsed events seemed to be under the guidance of her brother-in-law, Robert Fellowes, who remained the Queen's private secretary. In 1994, she traveled to Paris, and in early 1995, she made a four-day trip to Japan. Later, she traveled to Venice, Moscow, and Argentina.[7]

When Diana was not traveling the world and visiting with friends, she was often home alone at Kensington Palace, watching television or talking to friends on the phone.[8] Sometimes she stopped into the palace kitchen for a light supper with the chef.[9] She also worked out frequently with her personal trainer three mornings a week at a sports complex called Chelsea's Harbor Club. In addition, she swam at Buckingham Palace and visited a sport clinic where physical therapists helped her move her right knee, which had been injured earlier.[10] Her children spent less time with her following the separation from Charles. Because William was second in line for the throne, it was assumed that he needed the guidance of the royal family more than he needed guidance from his own mother.

Both Diana's chauffeur and her favorite bodyguard were reassigned to work for Charles. It seemed that Diana may have been feeling very alone when she spoke at a mental health conference in London later that year. "There seems to be a growing feeling of . . . emptiness in people's lives," she told the audience. "Deep within us all is a need to care and be cared for . . . yet many people, in their attempt to build a better life . . . lose touch with their own sense of belonging and of being a part of something greater than themselves."[11] Diana's remarks left people wondering about her private life.

"Two years ago, she was out nearly every night seeing friends," another friend told a *People* magazine reporter. "When she's seen now, she's nearly always alone or with one of her detectives. She's in desperate need of more true friends."[12]

Meanwhile, it seemed that friends came and went. Diana reportedly stopped visiting with de Lima when the ambassador's wife was interviewed by London's *Sunday Times* and expressed concerns about Diana's loneliness.[13]

Diana appeared to wander aimlessly in her personal life. William began to attend the private school Eton, and Diana knew that he would soon be more independent.[14] The press reported that Diana still struggled with bulimia and depression. "In public, Diana is terrific, but she has very dark moments when she cries her eyes out," said author Brian Hoey, who had written several books about the British royalty.[15]

As the months flew by, Diana and Charles apparently called a brief truce in their ongoing battles that were reported in London's newspapers. They took both their sons to Eton on William's first day there, arriving together in a Jaguar. At various other times in the weeks that followed, the two made public appearances together. Speculation began that, perhaps, a divorce would not occur. Charles, however, continued to be seen in public with Parker Bowles.[16]

Although Diana said little about getting a divorce, there was continued speculation that the royal couple would split

Prince William *(second from right)* is flanked by his estranged parents, the Prince and Princess of Wales, and is accompanied by his younger brother Prince Harry on his first day at Eton College on September 6, 1995. Prince William is the first future king of Britain to attend the venerable school, which has educated the sons of Britain's elite for more than 500 years.

permanently. In the meantime, Charles's popularity with the British people seemed to grow as he stepped up his own high-profile appearances.

Diana, however, could not allow Charles to gain the upper hand with the British press. She stayed in touch with her favorite reporters, although few outside of the media knew that she had ongoing relationships with the people who wrote stories about her and her failed marriage. At Kensington Palace, she entertained people in the media, including a reporter for the BBC, an editor for the London *Evening Standard*, and American newscaster Barbara Walters.[17] On her husband's forty-seventh birthday in 1995, Diana appeared in a British television interview, in which she admitted to the affair with Hewitt and told viewers that she thought that Charles was unfit to be king.[18] In addition, she talked of being bulimic and of self-mutilation, saying that she hurt her arms and legs.[19] After that interview, there were growing concerns that Diana suffered from some very deep problems.

Diana's private secretary at the time knew that the television interview was a huge mistake; however, he—and other members of the princess's staff—had no idea that the interview would be so scathing. The secretary and some of the other staff members resigned within the next few months.[20] They saw Diana as a manipulative woman who seemed to have no focus except, perhaps, to ruin the British monarchy.

Almost immediately, Britain's Conservative Party began to call for a royal divorce. "We do not want a running tit-for-tat between the two of them every year or so," said a spokesperson. "An amicable divorce with plenty of provision for the two boys is the only way out now."[21] The royal family acknowledged the interview but declined to announce a pending divorce. "We will of course be talking to the Princess to see how we can help her define her future role and continue to support her as a member of the Royal Family," the palace declared.[22]

Diana was clear with regard to her own intentions. "I'd like to be queen in people's hearts," she said during the television interview. "But I don't see myself as queen of this country. I don't think many people would want me to be queen. When I say many people, I mean the establishment that I married into."[23]

Although she said she did not want a divorce, Diana seemed destined to become the ex-wife of England's future king. Her attitudes and actions led to the couple's eventual permanent split. A month after that television interview aired, Queen Elizabeth encouraged Diana and Charles to divorce. "After considering the present situation the queen wrote to both the prince and princess earlier this week and gave them her view . . . that an early divorce is desirable," a palace spokesman said.[24]

In the ensuing months, Diana was a tough negotiator. She needed the palace's support so that she could continue to live with the protection and advantages that royal life offered her. In addition, the title that she would carry following her divorce was of great importance to her.

Four years after their official separation, the divorce of Diana and Charles was made official by London's High Court on August 29, 1996. Neither one appeared during the court process: Diana attended a luncheon sponsored by the English National Ballet, while Charles went to Balmoral, taking their two sons with him.[25]

Diana would remain a wealthy woman, according to the divorce settlement. She reportedly received a payment of $22 million and funds to run her office at Kensington Palace. She also retained her apartment at Kensington Palace. Charles was no longer responsible for paying Diana's bills, however—as stated in a letter that was sent to her 40 favorite stores.[26] The courts guaranteed a shared custody arrangement for their two sons; William was now 14, and Harry was 11.[27] Finally, in a move that infuriated Diana and many of the British people, the Queen stripped Diana of the title Her Royal Highness. She would retain only the title Princess of Wales.[28] The Queen also received permission for the divorce from the highest-ranking archbishop of the Church of England, so there would be no repercussions regarding Charles's position in the church or within the royal family.[29]

Diana's feelings, by that time, were very different from what they had been 15 years earlier, when she was married in a fairy-tale wedding. "You know, people think that at the end of the day, a man is the only answer," she said. "Actually, a fulfilling job is better for me."[30]

A NEW LIFE

Certainly, the calamity of the royal divorce and the media windstorm that followed it had stalled Diana's charitable efforts. Yet everyone, including the international press, seemed to know that Diana would not fade from the spotlight.

Months before her divorce, Diana had become involved with the international movement led by the Red Cross to rid the world of land mines. Her travels to Argentina and Pakistan, in support of this effort, drew worldwide acknowledgement. The anti-land mine crusade, which was becoming a worldwide effort, called for the passage of a treaty that would ban the production, export, and use of anti-personnel land mines.[31] One issue remained, however—Britain and the United States did not support such a treaty. The Red Cross estimated at the time that 300 million land mines were left unexploded around the world.[32] In January 1997, Diana went on a four-day visit to Angola to help publicize the international terror caused by land mines that were left behind after wars occurred. At the time, there were an estimated 9 million land mines in Angola alone.[33] The proliferation of the mines had resulted in 1 in every 334 Angolan citizens being amputees.

Diana rode past shanties in Angola, where local residents lived, and attended a workshop where dozens of men stood on their single, remaining legs. The princess met a 13-year-old girl at the workshop who had lost a leg when a bomb dropped from a plane as she walked to her parents' farm.

All of her previous months of personal suffering were immediately diminished for Diana. Here were people who no longer had all of their bodies, and they were survivors. Diana told members of the press, who followed the tour, that the stories of these victims were amazing and appalling.[34]

In addition to meeting victims of land mines, Diana also visited schools and women who nursed sick babies. During her tour, she realized that continuing her work with the international land mine movement would be a consuming project. "If I am to carry on with this anti-personnel mine issue, then there are many other countries which I will need to visit," she told a reporter.[35]

Later, Diana expressed her concerns about land mines to a reporter for the *Mirror*, a newspaper in London. "The world, with its many other preoccupations, remains largely unmoved by a death toll of something like 800 people every month—many of them women and children. Those who are not killed outright—another 1,200 a month—suffer terrible injuries and are handicapped for life," she said.[36]

Although the Queen had approved Diana's trip to Angola, in England there was some disagreement about the princess's stance on the issue. Some people thought she was trying to grab more headlines. Others thought she was going against the British and American governments—neither of which had decided to support a unilateral removal of mines. "Diana, because of her pulling power, has embarrassed the

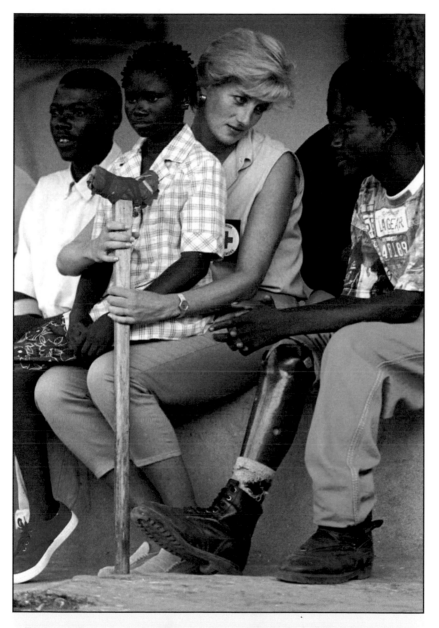

Diana talks to amputees at the Neves Bendinha Orthopedic Workshop on the outskirts of Luanda, Angola, on January 14, 1997. Sitting on Diana's lap is 13-year-old Sandra Thijica, who lost her left leg to a land mine while working the land with her mother in Saurimo, in eastern Angola, in 1994.

Government . . . because she supports those such as the Red Cross who deal with the horrific after-effects of landmines," one woman wrote in the *Independent* newspaper in London.[37]

Through her work with the Red Cross, Diana became involved with the International Campaign to Ban Landmines

INTERNATIONAL CAMPAIGN TO BAN LANDMINES

The International Campaign to Ban Landmines started in 1991 when several groups came together to discuss the issue of anti-personnel mines that littered the world. Those groups included Handicap International, Human Rights Watch, Medico International, Mines Advisory Group, Physicians for Human Rights, and Vietnam Veterans of America Foundation.

The organizations involved wanted an international ban placed on the use, production, stockpiling, and transfer of anti-personnel land mines. (Another type of land mine, the anti-tank land mine, requires the heavier weight of a vehicle to make it explode. This mine was not a part of the group's mission.) The ICBL requested, in addition, that countries begin a humanitarian effort to recover mines and to assist the victims—men, women, and children around the world—who have been hurt by their explosions.[*]

The organizations, at the time, were mainly concerned about mines in Africa, Asia, the Middle East, and Latin America. The ICBL immediately began to hold conferences and discussions regarding the land mine issue and how it should be dealt with on a global level. The campaign grew quickly, and today more than 90 countries are involved in it.

In 1997, the campaign and its then-coordinator, Jody Williams, won the Nobel Peace Prize for its work. A few

(ICBL). "ICBL was little known until Princess Diana made it her favorite charity this year, traveling to Bosnia and Angola on its behalf," said an article in *Newsweek*. Because of Diana's international influence, the movement might now spread to protect people around the world from being maimed by mines. Her visit to Angola, in fact, was turned

months later, the ICBL was able to get 122 governments to sign the Mine Ban Treaty at a meeting in Ottawa, Canada. (This is sometimes also called the Ottawa Treaty.) Other governments have signed the treaty since then (for a total of 136), but the United States, China, and Israel are among the 39 countries that have not. (Perhaps it was Diana's influence that caused the leaders of the United Kingdom to sign the treaty just after her death.)

In 1997, U.S. President Bill Clinton proposed the Demining 2010 Initiative, which set forth a different schedule of deadlines for clearing the world of land mines. Little progress, however, has been made since then regarding the United States' involvement in this issue.

Spreading its message of "Ban mines! Clear mines! Help the survivors!" the Campaign to Ban Landmines still exists around the world. In addition to banning and clearing the world of mines, the campaign calls for participation in the Mine Ban Treaty, the fencing off of minefields in various countries, and support for land mine survivors.

---

*"Global Ban on Landmines." Available online at http://www.ICBL.org.

into a television documentary that increased the land mine cause's profile.

The following June, Diana was one of the stars who attended a gala in New York to support the international cause. Elizabeth Dole, the president of the American Red Cross and the wife of presidential candidate Bob Dole, also supported the movement and oversaw the high-profile event. At home in London, Diana's participation in the anti-land mine movement grew.

"Even if the world decided tomorrow to ban these weapons, this terrible legacy of mines already in the earth would continue to plague the poor nations of the globe," she said at a London conference on the topic. "If an international ban on mines can be secured, it means, looking far ahead, that the world may be a safer place for this generation's grandchildren."[38] Diana expressed concern that the proliferation of land mines left over from past wars affected the poorest communities on Earth.

Later that month, however, Diana withdrew from a private meeting with anti–land mine supporters because she was once again being criticized by politicians in England. People thought that Diana was getting overly involved in a political issue. "She should make up her mind whether she is in the Royal Family or not," one politician said. "You can't have one foot in the Royal Family and one in the maelstrom of politics."[39]

Diana issued a statement, saying that she was not trying to be political but that she wanted to learn more about land mines. She said her involvement was only of a humanitarian nature. "The evening's all-party private meeting was to have been an opportunity for the princess to be further briefed on certain of the issues," said a statement issued by her office. "Details of the meeting have, however, now been made public and a political dimension has been introduced to its purpose. As a consequence the princess's attendance has been made untenable."[40] Despite the controversy, Diana's travels continued. She began to plan a trip to Croatia, where millions of mines had been left behind following the Bosnian War.

At the same time, and much more discreetly than her work with the land mine crusade, Diana began to see a new friend few people knew about: Hasnat Ahmad Khan, a Pakistani heart surgeon whom she had met at a London hospital when visiting a friend who had undergone surgery. They spent quiet moments at Kensington Palace or in out-of-the-way restaurants, getting to know each other. Diana would wear wigs and other disguises as she secretly left Kensington Palace on her way to meet him. She even planned a trip to visit a little-known charity to fight heart disease in Australia so that she and Khan could have some private time together in that country.

Diana, once again, began to think that she had found the man of her dreams. She wanted to marry a smart man who understood her position in life—as a princess and a traveling philanthropist. Just days after the land mine scuffle, a London newspaper announced that Diana had visited Pakistan and been accepted by the doctor's close-knit family.[41] It appeared that the two would be married. However, that was not the case. The surgeon, reportedly unprepared to deal with the very public life that Diana led, broke off the relationship a few weeks later.[42]

The self-proclaimed princess of people's hearts had just had her own heart broken.

The Fatal Accident

In early July, Diana accepted an invitation from the wealthy owner of Harrods department store, Mohamed Al Fayed, to visit his estate in the south of France. The reclusiveness of this sprawling Mediterranean estate would provide the security and serenity for which Diana longed. In addition, she was ready to leave London, where Prince Charles planned to honor Camilla Parker Bowles at a fiftieth birthday celebration later that month. Diana took her two sons and went away for a vacation.

Diana's failed relationship with Khan had left her rather distraught. A few days after she arrived at the Mediterranean estate, Mohammad's son, Dodi Al Fayed, showed up. It was the first time the two had met, and Diana seemed to take an instant liking to this carefree son of a billionaire.[1]

Following the trip, Diana had a busy summer; she spent weeks at a time with Dodi Al Fayed aboard his father's yacht, continued her work with the land mine campaign, and talked with friends about her own future. Her children were growing older, and Diana recognized that she had a lot of power and influence. She wanted to use it for important issues. As her sons went off with Charles for the rest of the summer, Diana was left to her own devices.

In June, Diana had met Jerry White when the organization he cofounded, the Landmine Survivors Network, helped sponsor a conference in London at which she spoke. Later in the summer, White and his cofounder, Ken Rutherford, visited Kensington Palace to talk to Diana about a trip they planned to take to Bosnia. White and Rutherford were not concerned only with Bosnia, however; they worried about mines throughout the world, including those in Cambodia, Afghanistan, Mozambique, Jordan, Eritrea, and Ethiopia. During this meeting at Kensington Palace, Diana suggested she join them on their Bosnian journey.[?]

The men agreed. In early August, the three of them— along with several others—traveled to Bosnia to visit people whose lives had been deeply affected by the proliferation of mines in that country. White later wrote in the *Christian Science Monitor*:

> Traveling with Diana on this remarkable trip, I repeatedly witnessed the princess's genuinely caring, almost magical way with everyone she met—from a 15-year-old girl . . . wounded by a landmine this year in Sarajevo, to a grieving young Muslim widow whose husband was killed in May, leaving her alone to raise their two young children.[3]

Diana visited victims in their homes, reached out to them, held their hands, and tried to ease their pain. "As a survivor of a land-mine blast, I'm not exaggerating to say the princess's touch was healing to those who met her," White said.[4]

LANDMINE SURVIVORS NETWORK

The Landmine Survivors Network was founded in 1997 by two men who had survived land mine explosions. Jerry White spent his junior year of college traveling abroad in 1984. While he was hiking with friends in Israel, he stepped on an unexploded mine and it blew off his right foot.

Nine years later, another American resident by the name of Ken Rutherford was working for a nonprofit organization in Somalia when his jeep hit a land mine; he lost both legs. The two men met several years later and eventually formed the Landmine Survivors Network.[*]

What is a land mine? Land mines are small explosive devices that lie on the ground or are slightly buried. They are primarily used in times of war to stop a vehicle or a person from being able to move forward. Yet, after a war ends, the unexploded mines usually are not recovered.

These devices have become a problem. They cause terrible injuries and kill people. It is estimated that unexploded land mines are spread across at least 70 countries around the world. Since 1975, at least one million people have been killed or maimed by land mines.

Princess Diana accompanied the Landmine Survivors Network during a trip to Tuzla, Bosnia-Herzegovina, just before she died in August 1997. White and Rutherford traveled with her as they worked to open the network's first office there. "Many people heard of LSN only because of Diana's involvement," White wrote

During the journey, Diana's passion touched many people. One man, who had lost two legs and most of his eyesight during a land mine explosion, was convinced that Diana possessed special gifts. "I don't think you need

on the organization's Web site. "She transformed landmines from a security issue into a humanitarian issue."[**]

The Landmine Survivors Network has a primary goal of helping the surviving victims of land mines receive good health care and become more independent. In addition, the network works hard to rid the world of mines. White and Rutherford were among the leaders involved with the International Campaign to Ban Landmines, which received the Nobel Peace Prize in 1997.

Although Diana's death was a huge loss for the organization, its members have continued to work toward its goals. In addition to its Bosnia-Herzegovina office, it has now established regional offices in Colombia, El Salvador, Ethiopia, Jordan, Mozambique, and Vietnam. The organization's many programs reach out to land mine survivors in 43 of the most-affected countries and regions in the world, including Iraq and Afghanistan.

Today, White is the executive director of the Landmine Survivors Network, which is based in Washington, D.C. Rutherford is an assistant professor of political science at Southwest Missouri State University and is a member of the network's board of directors.

---

[*]"Founders." Available online at http://www.landminesurvivors. org.

[**]"Princess Diana: Activist for Landmine Survivors." Available online at http://www.landminesurvivors.org/who_diana.php.

eyesight to see this type of beauty—after spending time with her, I sense it in her spirit," he said.[5]

Back in London, however, all was not well. As pictures of Diana's travels appeared in newspapers throughout the city, some people criticized her, saying that she should not dabble in the political issues surrounding mines. A French newspaper article made it sound like Diana criticized the British government for not taking a hard stance regarding the global cleanup of land mines left behind from past wars. Upon her return to London, she denied that she had criticized the British government. Again, Diana argued that her concerns with land mines were purely humanitarian, not political.[6] She attempted to stay clear of any political accusations; yet her actions spoke differently.

During the three-day trip to Bosnia, Diana talked with White and Rutherford about the group's next trip. She thought she might travel to Afghanistan and Cambodia in 1998. She and White made plans for him to visit her at Kensington Palace on September 5 so that they could discuss a speech she would give at an international meeting in Oslo, Norway, later that month. Diana had decided that she would not only campaign for a ban on the use of anti-personnel land mines, but she also wanted the treaty to include a message that victims would receive help as they attempted to rehabilitate their lives. White planned to take flowers to the September 5 meeting to thank her for the work she had done in Bosnia, but he never had the chance to do that.[7]

DIANA'S FINAL TRIP

In addition to Diana's growing concerns about land mines, she tried to find some comfort in her private life. She took a late-summer cruise with Dodi Al Fayed on his father's $32 million yacht. They stopped at ports along the French Riviera and stayed at a hotel on the northern coast of Sardinia, the second largest island in the Mediterranean Sea.

After a restful nine days, the two flew back to Paris aboard one of Mohamed Al Fayed's private jets. The pair checked into a suite at the Ritz, where Diana took the time to call one of the reporters who always wrote about her. Diana seemed elated, he later said. She told him that she planned to step away from some of her charity work—the latest controversy regarding her political land mine stance was apparently taking a toll.[8]

Diana ordered scrambled eggs with wild mushrooms and asparagus for dinner that night, when she and Dodi Al Fayed ate in the hotel's restaurant. Their dinner was interrupted, however, when they were told that their location had been discovered—a growing crowd of photographers was waiting outside the hotel entrance. The two returned to their suite and decided they would leave the hotel and head for Dodi Al Fayed's Paris apartment.[9]

The couple climbed into the backseat of a Mercedes that was driven by a member of the hotel's security staff named Henri Paul. Because Dodi's father owned the Ritz, the driver was familiar with the Al Fayed family. It was not revealed until days later that Paul had been drinking and that his blood-alcohol level was elevated above the point of sobriety. In the front seat with him was Dodi's bodyguard, Trevor Rees-Jones.

As some of the photographers reportedly followed them in cars and on motorcycles, Paul drove the car faster. He entered a tunnel along an expressway near the Seine River, at which point a gut-wrenching crash occurred. The Mercedes they were riding in hit a concrete support column, rolled over, and hit another wall. Paul's body leaned against the horn.[10] In the early morning hours of August 31, 1997, an eerie wailing was heard in the dark of night.

Some photographers took pictures with traditional cameras, but their film was later confiscated by investigators. Photographers screamed at each other, some made calls

The car *(right)* in which Diana was fatally injured when it crashed in the Pont d'Alma tunnel in Paris, France, on August 31, 1997. Diana, 36, was killed along with her companion, Dodi Al Fayed, 42, and their chauffeur Henri Paul, 41. A bodyguard, Trevor Rees-Jones, was the only survivor of the accident.

to their editors, and one opened the car door to check on its occupants.[11] Finally, ambulances arrived. Diana, whose heart was still beating, was rushed to a nearby hospital. By all reports of the evening, her heart stopped once and doctors revived her. It stopped a second time, and—although surgery was attempted—she died.

Diana, the Princess of Wales, was pronounced dead at 4:57 A.M. by the Interior Minister of France. Only Rees-Jones, the sole occupant of the car who wore a seatbelt, had survived the crash.

THE PEOPLE'S PRINCESS IS GONE

News spread quickly around the world. Details of the crash were issued from Paris throughout the night. Upon hearing of the accident, the BBC in Britain and news networks in the United States continued their broadcasts late into the evening.

Charles learned of Diana's death soon after it happened. He was at Balmoral with their sons, enjoying their traditional late-summer retreat. He fretted until morning, at which time he would have to tell his sons that their mother was dead.

At Kensington Palace, Diana's apartment was sealed by Paul Burrell, a butler with whom she was very close, and the palace's chauffeur. They wanted to make sure her private items were protected from anyone who entered. Burrell and the chauffeur then traveled to Paris to identify her body. They, too, were stunned at the news.[12] Diana's sisters arrived in Paris soon after the two royal employees did.

As her death was announced, people around the world began to mourn. Television anchors traveled to London and set up their camera crews for a week of painful coverage. People throughout the world turned on their televisions that morning to hear all of the details about the fateful crash.

Just after 7:00 A.M., Charles broke the news to his sons. They would not be seeing their mother, as previously planned, later that evening. She was dead, he told them. The boys were then reportedly whisked off—kept busy for the following few days at Balmoral, riding horses and hiking—to keep them away from London and the ongoing television reports of Diana's death. They stayed at Balmoral with their grandparents, Queen Elizabeth and Prince Phillip, while Charles flew to Paris to claim Diana's body.

As the royal family and palace staffers tried to deal with the startling news, mourners placed a growing mound of flowers at the entrance to Kensington Palace throughout that day and the following weeks.

Later in the day, Buckingham Palace released an official statement: "Buckingham Palace has confirmed the death of Diana, Princess of Wales. The Queen and the Prince of Wales are deeply shocked and distressed by this terrible news. Other members of the Royal Family are being informed. Details of the funeral arrangements have yet to be confirmed."[13]

Handmade signs began to appear next to the flower monument that grew. "Born a lady, became a princess, died a saint," said one.[14] The public outcry for Diana stunned the palace and overshadowed an internal struggle regarding plans for Diana's funeral. Services were immediately scheduled at churches around London, and flags were lowered to half-mast. Books of condolence were set up at St. James's Palace, where people waited hours to sign them.[15]

"The paparazzi pursued her everywhere, in the end to her death," said an article that appeared on September 1 in the *New York Times*.[16] In the early days following the accident, the photographers took all of the blame. After reports revealed the driver's blood-alcohol level, however, most accusations against the photographers were eventually dropped.

As the royal family and Diana's brother, now called Earl Spencer, discussed funeral arrangements, the rest of the world continued to mourn. Diana's brother argued that her sons should not be encouraged to walk behind their mother's coffin during the funeral procession, but Prince Charles disagreed. It was royal tradition, he reportedly told Earl Spencer.[17] Memorials of flowers grew—at Kensington, and then at Buckingham Palace, and even Althorp, the Spencer estate in northern England.

Princess Diana's funeral procession passes through London on its way to Westminster Abbey, on September 6, 1997. Following the gun carriage (*from left*) are Diana's father-in-law Prince Phillip, the Duke of Edinburgh; her son Prince William; her brother Charles, the ninth Earl Spencer; her son Prince Harry; and her former husband Prince Charles.

On the day of the funeral, the procession started at
Kensington Palace. When it passed by St. James's, Charles,
his father, the boys, and Diana's brother walked behind the
carriage and carried her coffin. Representatives of Diana's
favorite charities followed behind—those who suffered
from AIDS, victims of land mines, and officials from the
Red Cross.

The funeral was held on a Saturday, nearly a week after
the fateful accident. Prime Minister Tony Blair had chosen
Saturday for the funeral so that all citizens could watch the
very sad affair. The city of London nearly closed down so
that residents could say their final good-bye to the princess
they loved.

That morning, Queen Elizabeth gave a national television address. Wearing a black dress and pearls, she honored her daughter-in-law in a speech that Diana probably
would have been surprised to hear. "She was an exceptional
and gifted human being," said the Queen. "In good times
and bad she never lost her capacity to smile and laugh and
to inspire others with her warmth and kindness. I admired
and respected her for her energy and commitment to others, and especially for her devotion to her two boys."[18]

The funeral was held at Westminster Abbey. Once the
coffin was placed near the altar, Charles and his father placed
bouquets of white lilies near it. The coffin was adorned
with three wreaths of white flowers, which represented the
Spencer family, William, and Harry. A white card from her
sons had the word "Mummy" printed on it.[19]

Diana's sisters read poems, and her brother addressed
the crowd. Royalty, celebrities, and international politicians
such as Hillary Clinton and Henry Kissinger were seated
in the church. Famed entertainer Elton John performed a
heartbreaking rendition of his song "Candle in the Wind."
After the ceremony, a small procession left Westminster
Abbey and drove for two hours to a private ceremony at

Althorp. At her brother's request, Diana's remains were buried on an island there, where the estate's security measures would forever shield it from public viewing.[20]

TO HONOR THE PRINCESS

Ironically, the global gathering of land-mine treaty supporters in Oslo, Norway, was held just days later. By now, the United States and Britain were participating in the discussions. "The hundreds of delegates from 100 nations rose at the start of the conference for a moment of reflection on Diana's efforts to draw attention to the 26,000 people killed or maimed each year by landmines," the *New York Times* reported.[21] It was a moment, certainly, about which Diana would have been very pleased.

The princess's legacy would continue: The Diana, Princess of Wales Memorial Fund was established that month from the many donations made following her death. The fund makes grants to carry out Diana's work of championing charitable causes and humanitarian issues. Lady Sarah McCorquodale, the princess's eldest sister, is the president of the board of trustees.

A few weeks after Diana's death, the International Campaign to Ban Landmines and one of its founders, Jody Williams, were jointly awarded the Nobel Peace Prize. The organization's six-year campaign to bring attention to the worldwide problem was admittedly enhanced by Diana's participation. "The campaign is unstoppable now," said the spokesman for the United Nations Association in Britain. "Diana just swept people off their feet."[22]

Although Russia and Britain had joined the cause, the United States, China, and several other countries still did not participate. Nonetheless, the official international Mine Ban Treaty was signed in Ottawa, Canada, in 1997. Soon after the treaty was approved, Britain announced that it would commit $16 million to the clearance of land mines worldwide.[23]

Months later, a company in the United States caused public outrage when it emphasized the princess's association with the land mine issue and released a 15-inch Diana doll to the market. The doll was wearing a copy of the outfit Diana wore when she visited Angola's land-mine victims—jeans and a white blouse. "They're stealing the princess's image," complained a trustee of Diana's charity fund. "They're stealing from the very people she wanted to help."[24]

Diana's legacy continues, however, in people's minds and in the many books and articles written about her. "She was a terribly mixed up kid," said Jan Morris, a writer on *Time* magazine's Web site in 2001. "We felt close to her (when we were not infuriated by her) because she represented in herself so many of the worries our own children are likely to foist upon us—the disappointing school grades, anorexia and bulimia, unsuitable young men, a tendency to show off, a preoccupation with clothes and publicity, a rotten marriage, single motherhood and trouble with the in-laws."[25]

If she were alive today, Diana would likely say that her sons are her greatest legacy. Princes William and Harry have grown into productive young men. Prince William, who remains second in line to the British throne, was an officer in the British Army and Royal Navy and is now training to be a pilot in the Royal Air Force. His brother, Prince Harry, is a British Army officer and is third in line to the British throne.

On April 9, 2005, Prince Charles married Camilla Parker Bowles. She is now known as the Duchess of Cornwall and assists Charles and the royal family by making public appearances. Upon the announcement of their father's remarriage, William and Harry issued a joint statement on the royal family's Web site: "We are both very happy for our father and Camilla, and we wish them all the luck in the future." When, and if, Charles becomes the king of England, it is presumed that Camilla will be known as Her Royal Highness, the Princess Consort.[26]

The memory of Diana, Princess of Wales, will never fade away. On July 1, 2007, her sons honored her with a musical concert at London's Wembley Stadium on what would have been her forty-sixth birthday. "This event is about all that our mother loved in life—her music, her dancing, her charities and her family and friends," said William during opening remarks shared with his brother. Elton John then opened the show. It had been nearly 10 years since Diana's death.

Despite her prestige and her affluence, Diana lived a life that seemed to be a constant struggle. In the beginning, she was an innocent schoolgirl dealing with her own parents' divorce as she nursed dreams of marrying a prince. Once her wish came true, however, she realized that even the life of a princess was not perfect.

Diana's personal experiences in the world led to much self-discovery. Her struggle to overcome an eating disorder, her work with AIDS patients, and her compassion for land-mine victims had proven to her, and the rest of the world, that she had special talents. Her actions and travels placed a spotlight on charities and causes that otherwise might have gone unnoticed.

Although her relationship with photographers, reporters, and editors was tenuous and often stressful, Diana even formed bonds with the media. In fact, it was perhaps among the thousands of photographs that portrayed her in the press that the princess found her true self. She had become a confident woman with a powerful presence and the ability to give herself to others who had far greater needs than her own.

CHRONOLOGY

1961   Diana Frances Spencer is the third daughter born to Johnnie Spencer and Frances Roche Spencer on July 1 at Park House.

1969   Diana's parents divorce, and she is left to live with her father and her younger brother, Charles. Her mother remarries.

1970   Diana is enrolled in Riddlesworth Hall, which is located two hours away from her home.

1974   Diana is enrolled in West Heath, a boarding school that her two older sisters attended.

1975   Diana's father becomes the eighth Earl Spencer and moves into the family home known as Althorp; Diana visits him there during breaks from boarding school.

1977   Diana's father marries Raine Legge.

1978   Diana goes to a Swiss finishing school; she meets Prince Charles when her sister Sarah takes him to Althorp; in November, Diana is invited to attend the prince's thirtieth birthday party.

1980   Diana and Charles begin dating.

1981   Prince Charles asks Diana to marry him on February 6; the wedding is held on July 29.

1982   Prince William is born on June 21; he is the second in line to the British throne, behind his father.

1984   Prince Harry is born on September 16;
he is third in line to the British throne,
behind his father and his older brother.

1985   Diana and Charles take a highly publicized
trip to the United States, where Diana
dances with actor John Travolta during a
White House dinner.

1987   Diana's work with AIDS patients puts her
photograph in newspapers around the
world; her rising profile seems to make
her husband, the future king of England,
uncomfortable.

1990   Diana is the guest of honor at a charity
function in Washington, D.C., where
tickets cost $2,500 a person.

1991   Diana turns 30, and a London society
columnist calls her a "stunning success"
as a princess; Diana and Charles travel
together to Brazil.

1992   Diana's father dies in March; Andrew
Morton's noted biography *Diana: Her True
Story* is released (it is later revealed that
Diana was a source for the book); Charles
and Diana decide to officially separate
later that year at the request of Charles's
mother, Queen Elizabeth.

1993   Diana hires a speech coach to help her
prepare for many speeches around the
world; Diana also announces that she will
scale back her charity work.

1994   Diana travels alone to Paris, among other
places.

1995   Diana spends four days in Japan on a royal visit.

1996   Charles and Diana's divorce is made official; Diana begins work with the Red Cross to rid the world of land mines; she travels to Argentina and Pakistan.

1997   Diana continues her work, traveling to Angola with the International Campaign to Ban Landmines in January; in June, she meets Dodi Al Fayed and travels intermittently with him throughout the summer; she takes an early August trip to Bosnia with the Landmine Survivors Network; Diana and Al Fayed die in an automobile crash in Paris in the early morning hours of August 31.

NOTES

CHAPTER 1: JUST LIKE A FAIRY TALE

1. R.W. Apple Jr., "Amid Splendor, Charles Weds Diana," *New York Times*. July 30, 1981.
2. Cocks, Jay. "Magic in the Daylight," *Time*. August 3, 1981.
3. R.W. Apple Jr., "Charles and Lady Di Wed Today; Beacons Burn Across a Joyful Britain," *New York Times*. July 29, 1981.
4. Apple, "Amid Splendor, Charles Weds Diana."
5. Ibid.
6. Ibid.
7. Cocks. "Magic in the Daylight."
8. Tina Brown, *The Diana Chronicles*. New York: Random House, 2007, p. 39.
9. Ibid., p. 44.
10. Ibid., p. 56.
11. William Borders. "Prince Charles to Wed 19-Year-Old Family Friend," *New York Times*. February 25, 1981.
12. Andrew Morton, *Diana: Her True Story*. New York: Pocket Books, 1992, p. 88.
13. Stephen Barry, "Lady Diana Finds New House Rules Restrict Her Freedom," *Chicago Tribune*. August 19, 1985.
14. Ibid.
15. "Di's Private Battle," *People*. August 3, 1992.
16. John Skow, "Royalty vs. the Pursuing Press," *Time*. February 28, 1983.
17. Barbara Gamarekian, "On the Menu: Champagne, Dancing and Manners," *New York Times*. November 10, 1985.
18. Roland Flamini, "A New Di—The Princess of Wales Is a Royal Revelation," *Chicago Tribune*. September 17, 1989.

19. Roxanne Roberts, "Diana's the Draw—The Princess's Solo Washington Tour," *Washington Post*. October 4, 1990.

20. Lisa Anderson, "Wales Watching—Charles and Diana Seem Less Married and, Sadly, More Alike Than Ever," *Chicago Tribune*. June 16, 1981.

21. Ibid.

22. William D. Montalbano, "Princess Diana Admits Affair with a British Cavalry Officer," *Buffalo News*. November 21, 1995.

CHAPTER 2: A PRIVILEGED CHILDHOOD

1. Brown, *The Diana Chronicles*, p. 37.

2. Morton, *Diana: Her True Story*, p. 12.

3. Brown, *The Diana Chronicles*, p. 32.

4. "Winston Churchill: The Nobel Prize in Literature 1953." http://nobelprize.org/nobel_prizes/literature/laureates/1953/.

5. Morton, *Diana: Her True Story*, p. 30.

6. Ibid., p. 19.

7. Ibid., p. 21.

8. Brown, *The Diana Chronicles*, p. 40.

9. Ibid., p. 41.

10. Ibid., p. 40.

11. Morton, *Diana: Her True Story*, p. 26.

12. Allan Ramsay, "Unhappy Diana, By Her Brother," *Evening Standard*. October 5, 1992.

13. Morton, *Diana: Her True Story*, p. 29.

14. Ibid., p. 34.

15. Ibid., pp. 37–38.

16. Brown, *The Diana Chronicles*, p. 32.

17. Morton, *Diana: Her True Story*, p. 43.

18. Ibid., p. 46.

19. Ibid., p. 49.

20. Ibid., p. 52.
21. Brown, *The Diana Chronicles*, p. 69.
22. Jay Cocks, "Magic in the Daylight.," *Time*. August 3, 1981.
23. Brown, *The Diana Chronicles*, p. 75.
24. Ibid., p. 114.
25. Morton, *Diana: Her True Story*, p. 70.
26. Leonard Downie, Jr., "Pursuing the Prince—Charles' Bachelor Birthday," *Washington Post*. November 15, 1980.
27. Ibid.
28. "The Royal Newlyweds; She Charms with an Easy Grace," *New York Times*. July 30, 1981.
29. Brown, *The Diana Chronicles*, p. 133.
30. Ibid., p. 149.
31. Morton, *Diana: Her True Story*, p. 56.
32. Borders, "Prince Charles to Wed 19-Year-Old Family Friend."
33. Ibid.
34. Ibid.
35. Ibid.

CHAPTER 3: THE ROYAL WEDDING

1. Morton, *Diana: Her True Story*, p. 80.
2. "Buckingham Palace." http://www.royal.gov.uk/TheRoyalResidences/BuckinghamPalace/BuckinghamPalace.aspx.
3. Brown, *The Diana Chronicles*, p. 152.
4. Ibid., p. 154.
5. Ibid.
6. Jerene Jones and Andrea Chambers, "A Princess Bride Prepares," *People*. June 22, 1981.
7. Brown, *The Diana Chronicles*, p. 157.
8. Ibid., p. 151.

9. Leonard Downie Jr., "The Royal Wedding: Conversation Pieces: Engaging Interviews with Charles and Diana," *Washington Post*. July 29, 1981.

10. Ann Curry, "Diana Revealed: The Princess No One Knew," NBC News, 2006.

11. Downie, "The Royal Wedding: Conversation Pieces: Engaging Interviews with Charles and Diana."

12. Brown, *The Diana Chronicles*, p. 158.

13. Ibid.

14. Downie, "The Royal Wedding: Conversation Pieces: Engaging Interviews with Charles and Diana."

15. Cocks, "Magic in the Daylight."

16. Ibid.

17. Downie, "The Royal Wedding: Conversation Pieces: Engaging Interviews with Charles and Diana."

18. Ibid.

19. Cocks, "Magic in the Daylight."

20. R.W. Apple Jr., "Lady Diana Won't Vow to Obey Charles," *New York Times*. July 2, 1981.

21. Brown, *The Diana Chronicles*, p. 164.

22. Cocks, "Magic in the Daylight."

23. Morton, *Diana: Her True Story*, p. 91.

24. Brown, *The Diana Chronicles*, p. 166.

25. R.W. Apple Jr., "Charles and Lady Diana Wed Today," *New York Times*. July 29, 1981.

26. Ibid.

27. Brown, *The Diana Chronicles*, pp. 167–168.

28. Morton, *Diana: Her True Story*, p. 94.

29. Apple, "Charles and Lady Diana Wed Today."

30. Ibid.

31. Ibid.

32. Morton, *Diana: Her True Story*, p. 93.

33. Cocks, "Magic in the Daylight."

34. Appleton, "Lady Diana Won't Vow to Obey Charles."

35. Janice Castro, "The Vows Heard Round the World," *Time*. August 10, 1981.

36. Ibid.

37. Brown, *The Diana Chronicles*, p. 162.

38. Ibid.

39. Castro, "The Vows Heard Round the World."

40. Cocks, "Magic in the Daylight."

41. Apple, "Charles and Lady Diana Wed Today."

42. Ibid.

43. Ibid.

44. Ibid.

45. Ibid.

CHAPTER 4: AN HEIR AND A SPARE

1. Cocks, "Magic in the Daylight."

2. Leslie Berger, "The Honeymoon Cruise of Prince Charles and Diana," *Washington Post*. August 14, 1981.

3. Borders, "Prince Charles to Wed 19-Year-Old Family Friend."

4. Morton, *Diana: Her True Story*, p. 98.

5. Cocks, "Magic in the Daylight."

6. Ibid.

7. Jones and Chambers, "A Princess Bride Prepares."

8. Jay Cocks, "Queen for a New Day," *Time*. April 20, 1981.

9. Ibid.

10. Ibid.

11. Richard Stengel, "A Prince and His Princess Arrive," *Time*. November 11, 1985.

12. Cocks, "Queen for a New Day."

13. William Borders, "For Diana, Welsh Trip Is Triumph," *New York Times*. October 28, 1981.

14. Morton, *Diana: Her True Story*, p. 102.

15. Brown, *The Diana Chronicles*, p. 202.

16. Ibid.

17. Morton, *Diana: Her True Story*, p. 205.

18. John Skow, "Royalty vs. the Pursuing Press," *Time*. February 28, 1983.

19. Peter Osnos, "Prince William Conquers Britain," *Washington Post*. June 29, 1982.

20. R.W. Apple Jr., "Princess of Wales Has Boy: Charles Is 'Over the Moon,'" *New York Times*. June 22, 1982.

21. Ibid.

22. Ibid.

23. Ibid.

24. Osnos, "Prince William Conquers Britain."

25. Ibid.

26. Osnos, "Royal Heir Is Born," *Washington Post*. June 22, 1982.

27. Osnos, "Prince William Conquers Britain."

28. Morton, *Diana: Her True Story*, pp. 114–116.

29. Ibid., p. 117.

30. Skow, "Royalty vs. the Pursuing Press."

31. Ibid.

32. Morton, *Diana: Her True Story*, pp. 120–121.

33. Ibid.

34. Stephen Barry, "Royal Secrets—Life Behind the Palace Door," *Chicago Tribune*. August 18, 1985.

35. R.W. Apple Jr. "Princess of Wales Gives Birth to Her Second Son," *New York Times*. September 16, 1984.

36. Ibid.

37. "Wild About Prince Harry," *Washington Post*. September 17, 1984.

CHAPTER 5: THE PEOPLE'S PRINCESS

1. Michael White, "Dancing with Delight at Diana/US Royal Visit," *Guardian*. November 11, 1985.
2. Richard Stengel, "The Royal Couple Drops In," *Time*. November 18, 2005.
3. White, "Dancing with Delight at Diana/US Royal Visit."
4. V. Cook, "Diana's 'Wild' Dance," *London Telegraph*. November 11, 1985.
5. Stengel, "The Royal Couple Drops In."
6. Ibid.
7. Barbara Gamarekian, "Prince and Princess Encounter Elite in Dinner with 'Official' Washington," *New York Times*. November 11, 1985.
8. Stengel, "The Royal Couple Drops In."
9. Richard Stengel, "A Prince and His Princess Arrive," *Time*. November 11, 1985.
10. Barry, "Royal Secrets—Life Behind the Palace Door."
11. Ibid.
12. Barry, "Royal Secrets—Life Behind the Palace Door."
13. Stengel, "A Prince and His Princess Arrive."
14. Brown, *The Diana Chronicles*, pp. 280–281.
15. Ibid., p. 286.
16. Audrey Woods, "Princess Di: Queenly at 30," *San Francisco Chronicle*. June 27, 1991.
17. Sarah Lyall, "Once Just a Princess, Suddenly a Feminist," *New York Times*. November 26, 1995.
18. Morton, *Diana: Her True Story*, p. 128.
19. Ibid., p. 129.
20. Ibid., p. 132.
21. Ibid., p. 136.

22. Jo Thomas, "At Home, the Royal Couple Provoke an Unremitting Demand for Gossip," *New York Times*. November 9, 1985.

23. Ibid.

24. Scott Bolles, "Charles Brushes Up His Art," *Sunday Mail*. May 13, 1990.

25. Ibid.

26. Curry, "Diana Revealed: The Princess No One Knew."

CHAPTER 6: A MARRIAGE IN RUINS

1. Roberts, "Diana's the Draw—The Princess's Solo Washington Tour."

2. Ibid.

3. Ibid.

4. "Di Sneaks Extra Cuddles from the Kids," *Advertiser*. February 3, 1988.

5. Richard Cohen, "Checking Out with Princess Di," *Washington Post*. September 3, 1989.

6. Ibid.

7. Nicholas Moore, "5 Suicide Tries by Diana: Reported Book Portrays a Princess in Despair After Wedding," *Buffalo News*. June 7, 1992.

8. Bolles, "Charles Brushes Up His Art."

9. Ibid.

10. Associated Press-Reuters, "Prince Charles Breaks Arm in Tumble from Polo Pony," *Toronto Star*. June 29, 1990.

11. Lyall, "Once Just a Princess, Suddenly a Feminist."

12. Woods, "Princess Di: Queenly at 30."

13. Ibid.

14. Christopher Hitchens, "The Princess and the Fractured Fairy Tale," *Washington Post*. June 23, 1992.

15. "Will Charles Ever Get to Sit on the Throne?" *Toronto Star*. April 21, 1991.
16. Brown, *The Diana Chronicles*, p. 325.
17. "Will Charles Ever Get to Sit on the Throne?"
18. Brown, *The Diana Chronicles*, p. 326.
19. William E. Schmidt, "Charles and Diana Are Separating 'Amicably,'" *New York Times*. December 10, 1992.
20. Curry, "Diana Revealed: The Princess No One Knew."
21. Associated Press, "The 8th Earl Spencer Dies— Father of Princess Diana," *Washington Post*. March 30, 1992.
22. "Di Cries For Her Dead Father," *Herald Sun*. March 30, 1992.
23. Associated Press, "The 8th Earl Spencer Dies— Father of Princess Diana."
24. "Di Cries For Her Dead Father."
25. Brown, *The Diana Chronicles*, p. 343.
26. Ibid., p. 322.
27. Hitchens, "The Princess and the Fractured Fairy Tale."
28. Moore, "5 Suicide Tries by Diana: Reported Book Portrays a Princess in Despair After Wedding."
29. Schmidt, "Charles and Diana are Separating 'Amicably.'"
30. Ibid.
31. Ibid.
32. Ibid.
33. Ibid.
34. Martha Duffy, "The New Royal Watch," *Time*. December 21, 1992.
35. "Windsors' Royal Ruckus Continues," *USA Today*. December 7, 1992.

36. Duffy, "The New Royal Watch."
37. Eugene Robinson, "Prince Charles, Diana Will Separate," *Washington Post*. December 10, 1992.
38. Duffy, "The New Royal Watch."
39. Brown, *The Diana Chronicles*, p. 351.

CHAPTER 7: A JET-SETTING PHILANTHROPIST

1. Curry, "Diana Revealed: The Princess No One Knew."
2. Ibid.
3. Michelle Green, "The Outsider," *People*. December 6, 1993.
4. William Underhill, "The Princess Beats a Retreat," *Newsweek*. December 13, 1993.
5. Ibid.
6. Stephanie Mansfield, "Diana, in the New World— The Princess Wows Washington's Elite and Finds Haven from the Storm," *Washington Post*. October 22, 1994.
7. Michelle Green, "Going Public," *People*. November 6, 1995.
8. Green, "The Outsider."
9. Green, "Going Public."
10. Ibid.
11. Ibid.
12. Ibid.
13. Ibid.
14. Ibid.
15. Ibid.
16. Ibid.
17. P.D. Jephson, *Shadows of a Princess*, New York: HarperCollins, 2000, p. 429.
18. Brown, *The Diana Chronicles*, p. 396.

19. Martha Duffy, "Fractured Fairy Tale," *Time*. March 11, 1996.
20. Jephson, *Shadows of a Princess*, p. 449.
21. Sarah Lyall, "Diana's Soul-Baring Interview Draws Tory Calls for Divorce," *New York Times*. November 23, 1995.
22. Ibid.
23. Montalbano, "Princess Diana Admits Affair with a British Cavalry Officer."
24. Ann Gerhart, "Queen Elizabeth Urges Early Divorce for Charles and Diana—Prince Agrees That Marriage Should End, Palace Reports," *Washington Post*. December 21, 1995.
25. Fred Barbash, "To the Bitter End; The Famous Royal Marriage Dies Quietly," *Washington Post*. August 29, 1996.
26. Sarah Lyall, "It's Official: Charles and Diana Split, and She Pays Her Own Bills," *New York Times*. August 29, 1996.
27. Ibid.
28. Bernard D. Kaplan, "Queen Called 'Mean' to Diana: Monarch Under Fire for Taking Away Princess's Royal Title," *Gazette*. July 27, 1996.
29. Gerhart, "Queen Elizabeth Urges Early Divorce for Charles and Diana—Prince Agrees That Marriage Should End, Palace Reports."
30. Lyall, "Once Just a Princess, Suddenly a Feminist."
31. Suzanne O'Shea, "Princess's Landmine Crusade Close to Victory," *Scotsman*. September 18, 1997.
32. Ibid.
33. James Johnston, "Diana's Four-Day Visit to Angola," *Scotsman*. January 13, 1997.
34. Ruaridh Nicoll, "Diana Takes a Crusade to Angola," *Guardian*. January 15, 1997.

35. Ibid.

36. Kevin Maguire, "My Landmine Mission by Diana," *Mirror*. August 6, 1997.

37. Suzanne Moore, "Diana the Do-Gooder Versus the Bad Guys," *Independent*. January 17, 1997.

38. Valentine Low, "Now It's Diana the Serious and 'She Can Save Lives,'" *Evening Standard*. June 12, 1997.

39. "Princess Pulls Out of Meeting Following Attacks; Diana Steps on Publicity Mine," *Herald*. June 26, 1997.

40. Ibid.

41. Deborah Sherwood, et al. "Princess Diana, Her Heart Surgeon Hasnat and the Astonishing Family Summit that Sealed Their Love," *Sunday Mirror*. June 29, 1997.

42. Brown, *The Diana Chronicles*. p. 433.

CHAPTER 8: THE FATAL ACCIDENT

1. Brown, *The Diana Chronicles*, pp. 437–438.

2. Ibid.

3. Jerry White, "Travels with Diana: A Land-Mine Survivor's Tale," *Christian Science Monitor*. September 3, 1997.

4. Ibid.

5. Ibid.

6. Rachel Donelly, "Diana Denies Criticizing Tories Over Landmines," *Irish Times*. August 28, 1997.

7. White, "Travels with Diana: A Land-Mine Survivor's Tale."

8. "Taken Too Soon," *People*. September 15, 1997.

9. Ibid.

10. Ibid.

11. Brown, *The Diana Chronicles*, p. 443.

12. Ibid., p. 449.

13. Joe Garner, *We Interrupt This Broadcast*. Naperville, Ill.: Sourcebooks, 1998, p. 149.

14. "Taken Too Soon."

15. Ibid.

16. Anthony Lewis, "Out, Out, Brief Candle," *New York Times*. September 1, 1997.

17. Fiona Barton, "Why Earl Spencer Slammed Down the Phone on Prince Charles," *Sunday Mail*. November 8, 1998.

18. "'She Never Lost Her Capacity to Smile,'" *South China Morning Post*. September 6, 1997.

19. "The Day England Cried," *Newsweek*. January 22, 2008.

20. Ibid.

21. "Tribute to Diana at Land-Mine Talks," *New York Times*. September 2, 1997.

22. Mark Dowdney, "Her Nobel Cause," *Mirror*. October 11, 1997.

23. Anna Tomforde, "Princess Diana Conveyed the Landmine Problem to Ordinary People," *Deutsche Presse-Agentur*. October 10, 1997.

24. "Princess Di Doll Sparks an Outrage," *Belfast News Letter*. May 18, 1998.

25. Jan Morris, "The Naughty Girl Next Door," *Time*. June 24, 2001.

26. "Announcement of the marriage of HRH The Prince of Wales and Mrs Camilla Parker Bowles." http://www.princeofwales.gov.uk/mediacentre/press-releases/announcement_of_the_marriage_of_hrh_the_prince_of_wales_and__167.html.

BIBLIOGRAPHY

"Althorp Hospitality."Available online. URL: http://hospitality. althorp.co.uk.

"Althorp Living History." Available online. URL: http://www. althorp.com.

"Amid Splendor, Charles Weds Diana," *New York Times*. July 30, 1981.

Anderson, Lisa. "Wales Watching—Charles and Diana Seem Less Married and, Sadly, More Alike Than Ever." *Chicago Tribune*. June 16, 1981.

"Announcement of the Marriage of HRH The Prince of Wales and Mrs. Camilla Parker Bowles." Available online. URL: http://www.princeofwales.gov.uk/mediacentre/pressreleases/ announcement_of_the_marriage_of_hrh_the_prince_of_ wales_and__167.html.

R.W. Apple Jr., "Charles and Lady Diana Wed Today." *New York Times*. July 29, 1981.

———. "Princess of Wales Has Boy: Charles Is 'Over the Moon.'" *New York Times*. June 22, 1982.

———. "Princess of Wales Gives Birth to Her Second Son." *New York Times*. September 16, 1984.

Associated Press. "The 8th Earl Spencer Dies—Father of Princess Diana." *Washington Post*. March 30, 1992.

Associated Press-Reuters. "Prince Charles Breaks Arm in Tumble from Polo Pony." *Toronto Star*. June 29, 1990.

Barbash, Fred. "To the Bitter End; The Famous Royal Marriage Dies Quietly." *Washington Post*. August 29, 1996.

Barry, Stephen. "Lady Diana Find New House Rules Restrict Her Freedom." *Chicago Tribune*. August 19, 1985.

———. "Royal Secrets—Life Behind the Palace Door." *Chicago Tribune*. August 18, 1985.

Barton, Fiona. "Why Earl Spencer Slammed Down the Phone on Prince Charles." *Sunday Mail*. November 8, 1998.

Berger, Leslie. "The Honeymoon Cruise of Prince Charles and Diana." *Washington Post*. August 14, 1981.

Bolles, Scott. "Charles Brushes Up His Art." *Sunday Mail*. May 13, 1990.

Borders, William. "For Diana, Welsh Trip Is Triumph." *New York Times*. October 28, 1981.

———. "Prince Charles to Wed 19-Year-Old Family Friend." *New York Times*. February 25, 1981.

"Britain." *New York Times*. July 29, 1981.

Brown, Tina. *The Diana Chronicles*. New York: Random House, 2007.

"Buckingham Palace." Available online. URL: http://www. royal.gov.uk/TheRoyalResidences/ BuckinghamPalace/ BuckinghamPalace.aspx.

Castro, Janice. "The Vows Heard Round the World." *Time*. August 10, 1981.

Cocks, Jay. "Magic in the Daylight." *Time*. August 3, 1981.

———. "Queen for a New Day." *Time*. April 20, 1981.

Cohen, Richard. "Checking Out with Princess Di." *Washington Post*. September 3, 1989.

Cook, V. "Diana's 'Wild' Dance." *London Telegraph*. November 11, 1985.

Curry, Ann. "Diana Revealed: The Princess No One Knew." NBC News, 2006.

"Di Cries for Her Dead Father." *Herald Sun*. March 30, 1992.

"Di Sneaks Extra Cuddles from the Kids." *Advertiser*. February 3, 1988.

"Di's Private Battle." *People*. August 3, 1992.

Donelly, Rachel. "Diana Denies Criticizing Tories Over Land-mines." *Irish Times*. August 28, 1997.

Dowdney, Mark. "Her Nobel Cause." *Mirror*. October 11, 1997.

Downie, Leonard, Jr. "Pursuing the Prince—Charles' Bachelor Birthday." *Washington Post*. November 15, 1980.

———. "The Royal Wedding: Conversation Pieces: Engaging Interviews with Charles and Diana." *Washington Post*. July 29, 1981.

Duffy, Martha. "The New Royal Watch." *Time*. December 21, 1992.

———. "Fractured Fairy Tale." *Time*. March 11, 1996.

"Eating Disorders." Available online. URL: http://www.nimh. nih.gov/health/publications/eating-disorders/complete-publication.html.

"Fact Sheets and Brochures." Available online. URL: http://aids. gov/prevention/factsheets/index.html.

Flamini, Roland. "A New Di—The Princess of Wales Is a Royal Revelation." *Chicago Tribune*. September 17, 1989.

"Founders." Available online. URL: http://www. landminesurvivors.org.

Gamarekian, Barbara. "On the Menu: Champagne, Dancing and Manners." *New York Times*. November 10, 1985.

———. "Prince and Princess Encounter Elite in Dinner with 'Official' Washington." *New York Times*. November 11, 1985.

Garner, Joe. *We Interrupt This Broadcast*. Naperville, Ill.: Source-books, 1998.

Gerhart, Ann. "Queen Elizabeth Urges Early Divorce for Charles and Diana—Prince Agrees That Marriage Should End, Palace Reports." *Washington Post*. December 21, 1995.

"Global Ban on Landmines." Available online. URL: http:// www.icbl.org.

Green, Michelle. "The Outsider." *People*. December 6, 1993.

Hitchens, Christopher. "The Princess and the Fractured Fairy Tale." *Washington Post*. June 23, 1992.

Jephson, P.D. *Shadows of a Princess*. New York: HarperCollins, 2000.

Johnston, James. "Diana's Four-Day Visit to Angola." *Scotsman*. January 13, 1997.

Jones, Jerene, and Andrea Chambers. "A Princess Bride Prepares." *People*. June 22, 1981.

Kaplan, Bernard D. "Queen Called 'Mean' to Diana: Monarch Under Fire for Taking Away Princess's Royal Title." *Gazette*. July 27, 1996.

"Kensington Palace." Available online. URL: http://www.hrp.org.uk/KensingtonPalace.

Lewis, Anthony. "Out, Out, Brief Candle." *New York Times*. September 1, 1997.

Low, Valentine. "Now It's Diana the Serious and 'She Can Save Lives.'" *Evening Standard*. June 12, 1997.

Lyall, Sarah. "Diana's Soul-baring Interview Draws Tory Calls for Divorce." *New York Times*. November 23, 1995.

———. "Once Just a Princess, Suddenly a Feminist." *New York Times*. November 26, 1995.

———. "It's Official: Charles and Diana Split, and She Pays Her Own Bills." *New York Times*. August 29, 1996.

Maguire, Kevin. "My Landmine Mission by Diana." *Mirror*. August 6, 1997.

Mansfield, Stephanie. "Diana, in the New World—The Princess Wows Washington's Elite and Finds Haven from the Storm." *Washington Post*. October 22, 1994.

Montalbano, William D. "Princess Diana Admits Affair with a British Cavalry Officer." *Buffalo News*. November 21, 1995.

Moore, Nicholas. "5 Suicide Tries by Diana: Reported Book Portrays a Princess in Despair After Wedding." *Buffalo News*. June 7, 1992.

Moore, Suzanne. "Diana the Do-Gooder Versus the Bad Guys." *Independent*. January 17, 1997.

Morris, Jan. "The Naughty Girl Next Door." *Time*. June 24, 2001.

Morton, Andrew. *Diana: Her True Story*. New York: Pocket Books, 1992.

Nicoll, Ruaridh. "Diana Takes a Crusade to Angola." *Guardian*. January 15, 1997.

O'Shea, Suzanne. "Princess's Landmine Crusade Close to Victory." *Scotsman*. September 18, 1997.

Osnos, Peter. "Prince William Conquers Britain." *Washington Post*. June 29, 1982.

"Princess Di Doll Sparks an Outrage." *Belfast News Letter*. May 18, 1998.

"Princess Diana: Activist for Landmine Survivors." Available online. URL: http://www.landminesurvivors.org/who_diana.php.

"Princess Pulls Out of Meeting Following Attacks; Diana Steps on Publicity Mine." *Herald*. June 26, 1997.

Ramsay, Allan. "Unhappy Diana, by Her Brother." *Evening Standard*. October 5, 1992.

Roberts, Roxanne. "Diana's the Draw—The Princess's Solo Washington Tour." *Washington Post*. October 4, 1990.

Robinson, Eugene. "Prince Charles, Diana Will Separate." *Washington Post*. December 10, 1992.

Schmidt, William E. "Charles and Diana Are Separating 'Amicably.'" *New York Times*. December 10, 1992.

"She Never Lost Her Capacity to Smile.'" *South China Morning Post*. September 6, 1997.

Sherwood, Deborah, et al. "Princess Diana, Her Heart Surgeon Hasnat and the Astonishing Family Summit that Sealed Their Love." *Sunday Mirror*. June 29, 1997.

Skow, John. "Royalty vs. the Pursuing Press." *Time*. February 28, 1983.

Stengel, Richard. "A Prince and His Princess Arrive." *Time*. November 11, 1985.

———. "The Royal Couple Drops In." *Time*. November 18, 2005.

"Taken Too Soon." *People*. September 15, 1997.

"The Day England Cried." *Newsweek*. January 22, 2008.

"The Royal Newlyweds; She Charms with an Easy Grace." *New York Times*. July 30, 1981.

Thomas, Jo. "At Home, the Royal Couple Provoke an Unremitting Demand for Gossip." *New York Times.* November 9, 1985.

Tomforde, Anna. "Princess Diana Conveyed the Landmine Problem to Ordinary People." *Deutsche Presse-Agentur*. October 10, 1997.

"Tribute to Diana at Land-Mine Talks." *New York Times*. September 2, 1997.

Underhill, William. "The Princess Beats a Retreat." *Newsweek*, December 13, 1993.

White, Jerry. "Travels with Diana: A Land-Mine Survivor's Tale." *Christian Science Monitor*. September 3, 1997.

White, Michael. "Dancing with Delight at Diana/US Royal Visit." *Guardian*. November 11, 1985.

"Wild About Prince Harry." *Washington Post*. September 17, 1984.

"Will Charles Ever Get to Sit on the Throne?" *Toronto Star*. April 21, 1991.

"Windsors' Royal Ruckus Continues." *USA Today*. December 7, 1992.

"Winston Churchill: The Nobel Prize in Literature 1953."Available online. URL: http://nobelprize.org/nobel_prizes/literature/laureates/1953/.

Woods, Audrey. "Princess Di: Queenly at 30." *San Francisco Chronicle*. June 27, 1991.

FURTHER RESOURCES

BOOKS

Anderson, Christopher. *After Diana: William, Charles, and the Royal House of Windsor.* New York: Hyperion, 2007.

Brown, Tina. *The Diana Chronicles.* New York: Broadway Books, 2007.

Jephson, Patrick. *Portraits of a Princess: Travels with Diana.* New York: St. Martin's Press, 2004.

McDowell, Colin. *Diana Style.* New York: St. Martin's Press, 2007.

Morton, Andrew. *Diana: Her True Story.* New York: Pocket Books, 1992.

———. *Diana: Her New Life.* New York: Simon & Schuster, 1994.

People editors. *Diana, An Amazing Life: The People Cover Stories, 1981–1997.* New York: People, 2007.

WEB SITES

Althorp
  http://www.althorp.com/

Concert for Diana
  http://www.concertfordiana.com/

Diana: A Celebration
  http://www.dianacelebration.com/

Historic Royal Palaces
  http://www.hrp.org.uk/

The Diana, Princess of Wales Memorial Fund
  http://www.theworkcontinues.org/

The Official Web Site of the British Monarchy
  http://www.royal.gov.uk/

The Prince of Wales Web Site
  http://www.princeofwales.gov.uk/

PICTURE CREDITS

INDEX

ABOUT THE AUTHOR

SHERRY BECK PAPROCKI has recently written several juvenile biographies for Chelsea House, including *Oprah Winfrey: Talk Show Host and Media Magnate* (2006), which was placed on the Nonfiction Honor List created by the Voice of Youth Advocates (VOYA); *Ellen DeGeneres: Entertainer* (2009); and *Martha Stewart: Lifestyle Entrepreneur* (2009). Her other juvenile biographies include those about Bob Marley, Vicente Fox, Katie Couric, and Michelle Kwan. She is the editor of *Columbus Monthly Homes* and coauthored *The Complete Idiot's Guide to Branding Yourself* (Penguin, 2009) with her husband, Ray Paprocki. Her bylines have appeared in *Preservation* magazine, the *Chicago Tribune*, the *Cleveland Plain Dealer*, *Los Angeles Times Syndicate*, and others. She is a graduate of the Ohio State University School of Journalism and is a senior lecturer at Otterbein College. She is the mother of two adult children.